ILLUMINATE THE WAY

CHASE MIELKE

ILLUMINATE THE WAY

The School Leader's Guide to Addressing and Preventing Teacher Burnout

ascd

Arlington, Virginia USA

2800 Shirlington Road, Suite 1001 • Arlington, VA 22206 USA
Phone: 800-933-2723 or 703-578-9600 • Fax: 703-575-5400
Website: www.ascd.org • Email: member@ascd.org
Author guidelines: www.ascd.org/write

Richard Culatta, *Chief Executive Officer;* Anthony Rebora, *Chief Content Officer;* Genny Ostertag, *Managing Director, Book Acquisitions & Editing;* Susan Hills, *Senior Acquisitions Editor;* Mary Beth Nielsen, *Director, Book Editing;* Megan Doyle, *Editor;* Thomas Lytle, *Creative Director;* Donald Ely, *Art Director;* Katelynne Vizcayno/The Hatcher Group, *Graphic Designer;* Valerie Younkin, *Senior Production Designer;* Circle Graphics, *Typesetter;* Kelly Marshall, *Production Manager;* Shajuan Martin, *E-Publishing Specialist;* Christopher Logan, *Senior Production Specialist*

PAPERBACK ISBN: 978-1-4166-3223-8 ASCD product #123032 n8/23
PDF E-BOOK ISBN: 978-1-4166-3224-5; see Books in Print for other formats.
Quantity discounts are available: email programteam@ascd.org or call 800-933-2723, ext. 5773, or 703-575-5773. For desk copies, go to www.ascd.org/deskcopy.

Library of Congress Cataloging-in-Publication Data

Names: Mielke, Chase, author.
Title: Illuminate the way : the school leader's guide to addressing and preventing teacher burnout / Chase Mielke.
Description: Arlington, Virginia, USA : ASCD, [2023] | Includes bibliographical references and index.
Identifiers: LCCN 2023014081 (print) | LCCN 2023014082 (ebook) | ISBN 9781416632238 (paperback) | ISBN 9781416632245 (pdf)
Subjects: LCSH: School management and organization—United States—Psychological aspects. | Educational leadership—United States. | Teachers—Job stress—United States. | Teaching—Psychological aspects. | Burn out (Psychology)—Prevention. | Stress management.
Classification: LCC LB2805 .M465 2023 (print) | LCC LB2805 (ebook) | DDC 371.1001/9—dc23/eng/20230505
LC record available at https://lccn.loc.gov/2023014081
LC ebook record available at https://lccn.loc.gov/2023014082

31 30 29 28 27 26 25 24 23   1 2 3 4 5 6 7 8 9 10 11 12

To Ashlee,
You are the spark of this book and my life.

ILLUMINATE THE WAY

THE SCHOOL LEADER'S GUIDE TO ADDRESSING AND PREVENTING TEACHER BURNOUT

Introduction

"I'm not asking you to die for your students. I'm asking you to *kill* for your students."

I expected our active shooter training to be heavy. But I didn't expect these words from our training officer. Nor did I expect to hear so much silence, punctuated with sniffling noses—adults sucking back the emotions that leak when the audio of the Columbine shooting blasts across the auditorium. Gut-dropping sadness of gunshots outside a librarian's door. Empathetic fear when she tells students that it's going to be OK, not knowing or not showing that kids were being killed on the other side of the wall.

Next came the active shooter simulation. I was required to play the role of a teacher—my colleagues played my students. In the middle of a mock lesson, an officer acted as an active shooter, firing off blanks in the hallways. Others simulated children getting shot at, scrambling, screaming, pounding on doors as we locked them in (or out) within seconds.

The shooter screamed my name, "Mr. *Mielke*! Come out or I'll shoot everyone in this hallway!" asking me to unlock the door or he will kill. But I followed the protocol: You don't unlock a door for anyone. Not even if it is your own child. More blanks shot off. More screams outside. Shaking behind a barricaded door with a baseball bat. Wondering how teaching got to this point.

Kill for your students.

No college instructor, no mentor, no administrator or trainer had ever told me—ever knew—that being a teacher today might require me to kill an active shooter. To triage a suicidal student. To tactfully teach amid tense social and political issues like racism and gender norms and mask mandates.

Yet this is what we are asked to do. We are asked to do more than talk about content we love or assess student knowledge or create strategic interventions. We are asked to forgive a child after she has screamed profanity at us. We are expected to flex our thinking and strategies on a night's notice when a virus threatens our own families.

This is not bemoaning that teachers can't handle these things. Clearly we have. Clearly we will. I'm not even claiming that we *shouldn't* be well-trained on how to handle school shootings and pandemics.

But this is a gut check: How well-equipped are our school leaders to help teachers manage the *emotional* elements of teaching today? How knowledgeable are we on the real factors contributing to exhaustion and cynicism and inefficacy? How skilled are we at helping our teachers build resilience and maintain purpose when their students experience trauma or their next month of teaching shifts to remote instruction or they are asked to *kill for their students*?

For too long, our culture has prioritized the cerebral experience of educators over the social-emotional. We've spent billions on new curriculum and learning management systems and trainers to teach teachers how to ask better questions or unpack standards. We've dismissed teacher stress as distractions and annoyances from our work. *Suck it up and put on a happy face because your students* need *you.*

Put differently, we've focused on teacher *effectiveness* at the expense of teacher *affectiveness*: the social-emotional conditions of a teacher's motivation, resilience, purpose, and problem solving. But we can't have effectiveness without affectiveness. We cannot have rigorous curricula without resilient educators. We can't boost achievement amid burnout and exhaustion. We don't improve the quality of education until we improve the working conditions of educators. But don't take my word for it: look at the data.

Follow the Smoke

For years, educators (and education researchers) have been sounding the alarm on teacher burnout. But the alarm is no longer a proactive suggestion—a "hey, it might storm later." It is now a reactive scream— "a tornado is dismantling your house." A 2022 Merrimack College Teacher Survey found that 44 percent of teachers are likely or very likely to leave their job within the next two years—up from 29 percent in 2011 (Kurtz, 2022). Maybe not all of those teachers leave, but if even half of them do, that means nearly a quarter of your staff will be gone in a couple years; teachers with 3–9 years' experience are the most likely to leave.

And the talent reservoir is running dry. According to the Economic Policy Institute, by 2025, there will be a demand of over 300,000 teachers to fill positions; however, the projected supply is expected to be just over 100,000, suggesting that two-thirds of positions may not be filled (Garcia & Weiss, 2019). While other educational researchers are skeptical, citing that the stats are often overblown, there is a growing issue of finding qualified candidates. Another study conservatively estimated 36,000 vacant positions in August 2022, but 163,000 positions were held by underqualified educators teaching without certification or outside their subject area (Nguyen et al., 2022). The talent pool is cracked, and the water supply isn't strong enough to refill it.

Attrition isn't the only issue. Teachers who stay may be burned out beyond effectiveness. For those teachers who stay, only 12 percent of teachers say they are highly satisfied with their work, *five times* less than in 2008. Another study found that, since 2020, two thirds of teachers had increased levels of exhaustion and inefficacy, and half had increased levels of cynicism—hallmarks, we will see, of burnout (Bartlett, 2021).

OK, you probably didn't *need* to look at data to know that burnout is affecting education. You see this when job postings that used to produce hundreds of candidates now yield just a few (who hopefully at least filled out the application correctly). You see this in the special education position that you can't keep filled. You see it as your colleagues quit midyear and switch to new careers.

Teacher burnout is the minor tweak to a daily schedule that unleashes a flood of angry emails and angsty office visits from your staff.

It's a teacher who used to thrive with new challenges and offer ideas suddenly going cold, stuck in fatigue and a fixed mindset.

It's that moment when you want so badly for a colleague or teacher to shift their thinking—to embrace a new strategy, to reflect on a lesson, to consider a new approach, to *stop being so cynical!* Instead, there is defensiveness, justification, downright obstinance . . . and more cynicism.

The erosion of teacher well-being is leading to landslides of loss affecting more than a school's ability to fill a position. An educator's burnout ripples out to the entire school system—creating more cynical cultures, increasing costs due to absenteeism and hours spent hiring, and, most important, creating worse learning outcomes for students.

If we stand any hope of creating thriving schools, it begins by creating thriving teachers. We will not become more effective with our work until we empower our staff to build greater affectiveness. Although the stats and experiences in schools may seem dire, the fires of purpose and desire still exist in our schools. Students still need teachers and teachers still show up every day looking to make a difference—to do this great work we call education. But educators need help to reignite their reasons and resilience. They need the permission, skills, and structures to be more *affective.*

The Goal of This Work

When I share the debilitating effects of burnout—of in*affective* educators—with school leaders in speeches and workshops and individual meetings, without fail a deliberating devil's advocate starts up: *There is no way I can (or should) try to make everyone happy all the time.* Which leads us to an unfortunate element baked into our educational culture: toxic positivity—the unhealthy belief that everyone must be happy all the time. Toxic positivity is not only unrealistic and unhealthy but also rejected by teachers and administrators alike. It puts unrealistic pressure that teachers have to suck it up and put on a happy face—that school leaders need to approach issues with laissez-faire policies and campfire talks.

Happiness is not the goal. We can't be happy all the time, nor should we try. The goal is developing skills, strategies, and cultures that are resilient—the ability to maintain and savor what's good and bounce back with purpose when things aren't. When I describe an *affective* educator, I'm describing someone who has

- A strong level of autonomy and internal locus of control.
- High self-efficacy in diverse teaching contexts.
- Resiliency skills for tackling individual and group challenges.
- Awareness of when and how to regulate diverse emotions.
- Intrinsic motivation to grow oneself, one's students, and one's team.
- Positive relationships with students, colleagues, administration, and families.

Affectiveness isn't the same as "happy." Our Greek history nerds know that there's a difference between hedonia (pleasure) and eudaimonia (purpose). Affective teachers want purpose more than pleasure, agency more than ease, and depth more than peace. Without a doubt, joy, fun, and relaxation don't abound in today's schools, but building an affective culture doesn't mean trying to make everyone happy or ignoring the worthwhile challenges of education. Absolutely, there are barriers, policies, and approaches that cause undue stress for teachers, and we'll explore these. But affective teachers don't need (or want) pampering—they want the support, conditions, and skills that allow them to maximize the purposeful work they do.

So, what do we do to build affective teachers? We can't do as many schools have for years: ignore the concept entirely (i.e., *suck it up*). Our statistics and experiences show that schools are hemorrhaging from unresolved educator burnout and attrition. But we also can't treat these issues as *just* issues of "self-care." You'll learn very quickly through this book that burnout is an issue of organizations, not individuals. Thankfully, decades of research are illuminating the path.

There are clear symptoms, causes, and solutions to burnout. It's time to step out of the dark and into the light.

Fueling the Solution: Learn the What of Burnout and the How of Thriving

For over a decade and half, I've dedicated my personal and professional lives to understanding not just the science of human thriving but also the application of the research in schools. I've traveled the world, speaking to and training students, teachers, parents, and school leaders to understand how individual and collective well-being (or lack of) affect every element of the work of schools. I've developed and taught award-winning classes on positive psychology, leadership, and interpersonal communication. I've coached teachers of all levels and developed school improvement plans and professional development within my school district and beyond. But most of all, I've done the heavy lifting so you don't have to (or have time to); I've pored through the peer-reviewed research, reflected on my own experiences in teaching and leadership, and helped put theories into practice. I've had candid conversations with teachers and administrators of all experience levels in rural, suburban, and urban districts—before, during, and after COVID-19 rattled education to its roots.

Through this decade and a half of living educator well-being, I'm convinced that every school leader needs to know three things to bolster teacher effectiveness *and* affectiveness:

- The three dimensions of burnout.
- The six biggest causes of burnout.
- The three positive approaches to more affective schools.

This book is built around these three goals: to help you identify the what and why of burnout and the how of helping educators not just survive this profession but thrive.

Though the World Health Organization recently deemed burnout an occupational hazard in the International Classification of Diseases, individual and organizational burnout has been researched and understood for decades. Michael Leiter and Christina Maslach, experts on burnout, have identified three dimensions of burnout: exhaustion, cynicism and inefficacy. These dimensions are the well-established symptoms of burnout, but the causes are also well-validated (Maslach & Leiter, 2000).

But this is critical: If the flame inside your educators is burning out, we can't only block the wind or the conditions killing the fire. We must fuel the spark. We must give the fire what it needs to not just flicker but blaze. A central tenet of this book is that well-being is not solely the absence of bad; it's the presence of good. Decades of psychological and organizational research have shown that we must *both* eradicate the causes of languishing *and* promote the conditions of well-being (Seligman, 2004). Satisfaction is not the opposite of dissatisfaction—different elements of our work affect both (Herzberg, 1964). To fuel our educators, we will draw on the research of Deci and Ryan, who have demonstrated that three psychological needs shape our motivation and well-being: autonomy, relatedness, and competence.

Here's how we're going to rebuild the fire that is flickering inside your colleagues and staff:

We'll begin by helping you upgrade your understanding of burn-out: Well-being 2.0. I'll unpack an easy-to-understand analogy of why burnout is an issue of organizations, not individuals. You'll learn that the status quo effort of giving teachers "self-care strategies" won't give individuals or schools the power they need to perform at our best level. You'll see burnout in a whole new light.

In Chapter 2, I'll equip you with the Illuminating Mindsets: four actionable mental frames that great school leaders adopt to transform the affectiveness *and* effectiveness of their staff. You'll see how these mindsets can work as a process to draw insights, create solutions, and build the collective efficacy of teams. These mindsets will allow you not only to reignite your educators' dedication to this work but also illuminate as a source of hope, strategy, and success for a better future for schools.

In Chapters 3, 4, and 5, we will begin to examine the Affectiveness Continuums, first exploring the Distressed/Empowered continuum (see Figure I.1). We will understand the effects of emotional exhaustion and its primary causes: work overload and lack of autonomy.

FIGURE I.1

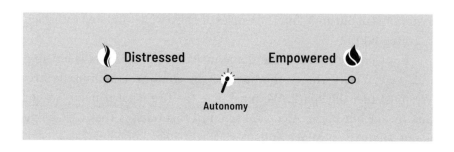

Our power move will be leveraging *autonomy*: giving educators the time, resources, and trust to take control of their work, overcoming stress, increasing efficiency, and creating more impactful moments for students.

In Chapters 6 and 7, we look at the Disconnected/Engaged continuum (see Figure I.2). We'll learn that symptoms of burnout like cynicism and depersonalization are defense mechanisms drawn from distinct causes. Rather than telling people to "stop being so negative all the time," we'll double down on the power of positive social *relatedness*, using six social skills to create trusting and cohesive cultures.

Last, in Chapters 8 and 9, we do a deep dive into the Defeated/Efficacious continuum (see Figure I.3). We'll look at the four roots of efficacy, why efficacy is so important for our staff and students, and

FIGURE I.2

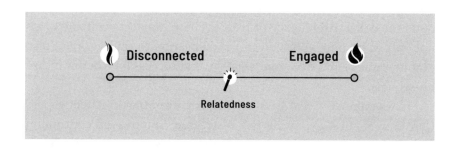

FIGURE I.3

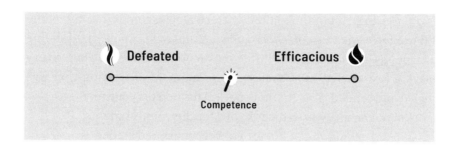

how to build *competence* in strategic ways—no matter what a person's experience or skill set.

Why You, Why Now

If you've made it this far, you may still be wondering, *Why now? There are so many things to do in education: curricula to revamp, PD to plan, meetings to attend. How can I justify time to focus on educator well-being?* If you give me a chance, I'll show you why educator well-being is the X-factor of high-performing schools—how being at our best helps us *give* our best to the students who need it. But until then, I ask you to flip the question. Don't ask what you gain by prioritizing educator wellness; ask what you *lose* if you don't. Who will implement that curricula with the passion it deserves if educators are exhausted? How do you develop your professionals with a rotating door of attrition each year, each month, and each day? What meetings will matter when the room is filled with cynicism and distrust? What good is a school with empty hallways and absent classrooms? There is no greater time to improve educator well-being because the future of schools will blaze or extinguish based on the engagement, empowerment, and efficacy of our educators. And the flame is stifling.

If you're holding this book, there's a reason. Either you or someone you know realized that you have influence. Whether you are a top-level decision maker or a discount-boots-on-the-ground school worker, your actions ripple out to the world around you (I'll prove it).

Whether you make policy changes that affect thousands of educators or conversations that help one, your greatest weapon against burnout is greater understanding paired with strategies and effort. So, while I'll use terms like *school leader* and *staff* and *team*, know that I define a leader as anyone who has influence on others (which is you). Every blazing fire started as a small spark, a moment of ignition that was fueled and tended. You are that spark. This book is your fuel.

I'm not asking you to die for your teachers and students.

I'm not asking you to kill for your teachers and students.

I'm asking you to breathe life into the most critical profession in the world—to reignite our purpose for doing this work—to illuminate the path to a brighter future for every colleague and every student in your life.

Let's let the sparks fly.

PART I

The Illuminating Leader

1

Educator Well-Being 2.0

Ashlee is a veteran teacher at a Title I elementary school. Despite the many challenges her students face, her students meet or exceed grade-level growth goals. She holds a master's degree in curriculum and instruction, is consistently rated as a highly effective teacher, and has received a county "Outstanding Educator" award. She is compassionate. Kind. Creative. Intelligent.

And she's burning out—considering each day whether she wants to stay in education.

She also happens to be my wife.

I travel and present to educators all over the world about educator burnout, highlighting the research-based strategies that have helped me and tens of thousands of educators strengthen well-being.

So why is my wife—a phenomenal teacher—burning out? She has access to a guy who can cite and teach ad nauseum the strategies that lead to increased gratitude, purpose, and joy. I can do a deep dive on why exercise and mindfulness and forgiveness boost our physical and emotional health. I can help her spot every cognitive distortion that arises and smite it with a research-based reframe. But it's not enough.

Because burnout isn't about the individual—it's about the organization. It is an issue of *context*, not *character*.

My wife is a testament to how we—myself included—have misunderstood burnout, placing the onus on teachers via "self-care solutions." If we want to reduce burnout, though, it will take more than exercise initiatives, meditation apps, and free donuts in the staff lounge. More than cognitive reframes and mindfulness strategies. Much more.

Let's start with a better understanding of what leads to teacher burnout.

The Computer Analogy

My generation is the last generation to have experienced childhood before the technology boom of high-speed internet and smartphones. I have the nostalgic stress of screeching dial-up internet sounds. Of loading Napster and initiating the lethargic download of one Dave Matthews Band song and praying it finishes the download by the time I get home from school. (Sorry about tying up the phone line, Mom. Making a sappy mixed CD for Audrey was more important.) Though technology has come a *long* way in the past few decades, there is one constant that will never change: technology can let us down.

Think about the last time that a computer failed you. Maybe it crashed unexpectedly. Perhaps it was a Wi-Fi glitch or unexpected browser reboot. Maybe the whole machine started whirring and working up heat like it was about to explode. As you consider a computer failure, think about what was at fault. Was it the software or the hardware? Was it a virus or a low battery?

We're going to look at teacher burnout through the lens of a computer (see Figure 1.1). I have an obligatory caveat that teachers—humans—are much more complicated than computers (and can't be replaced by them). But this analogy will get us started.

The Charger: Self-Care Strategies

One of the first efforts school leaders use to support staff well-being is promoting self-care. Exercise competitions, meditation websites, wellness workshops. To many, this seems like the logical move: the teacher is burning out, so fix the teacher. But, as we will see

FIGURE 1.1

The Computer Analogy

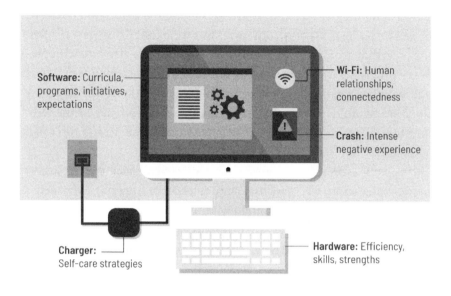

over and over, burnout is the product of working conditions. Asking teachers to fix their burnout is like asking a seed to grow better when the soil is dry and the sun is nowhere to be found.

We shouldn't ignore the importance of self-care. Educators benefit when they use research-based practices to improve their well-being (Mielke, 2019). We need energy and motivation to "turn on" our skills. But self-care is like the charger and battery of a computer. A teacher can have all the self-care strategies in the world and be fully charged, but damaged hardware or running too much software will zap energy. Our experience with vacations and breaks points to this. If we recharge when we're away from work but lose energy in days or weeks without another break (e.g., "February Funk"), then burnout is not an issue of limited self-care strategies. Put differently, we must address the systems, policies, and conditions that "drain batteries" so quickly and reliably. We have to look at the software and hardware.

The Software: Systems (Curricula, Programs, Initiatives, Expectations)

Running too much software at once is a surefire way to crash or slow a computer. If we want to avoid draining the battery on our computers or phones, we close out programs we're not using—even delete the ones that aren't serving a purpose anymore. We also know that the fewer programs we have running, the better the performance on each one, whether we're talking about computers or workers. The key questions are twofold: How many programs are we running at a time? And how inefficient are our systems because we're trying to run too much at once?

As we'll explore later, work overload is the biggest cause of emotional exhaustion, the first major dimension of burnout (Maslach & Leiter, 2000). I've seen this unfold with my wife. She showed me all the scripted curriculum guides she has to use in her elementary school—seven in total, three brand new. Her day is mapped out nearly minute to minute, a note from administration reading, "You won't have time for a scheduled snack, so try to build one in with your students while they work." In my wife's words, "I feel like I have no time to do the things that made me love teaching."

The Hardware: Efficacy

OK, maybe you *have* to run a few initiatives at the same time to try to make gains. If so, you'll need to improve the hardware to keep up with the energy and focus demands. Just as improving computer hardware takes more time and effort than adding software and programs, improving the hardware of educators is an investment. It takes high-quality coaching, feedback, and positive support.

Inefficacy is another major dimension of burnout (Maslach & Leiter, 2000). Building efficacy requires more than confidence-building mantras like "You got this!" and "We value you!" It requires mastery experiences: competence attained through high-quality professional development and timely, constructive feedback in safe, supportive environments. If we want teachers to persevere through challenges, we need to invest in the conditions that build efficacy and involve coaching, time, and support.

The Wi-Fi: Connectedness

"Teachers, our internet is down. We will notify you when it is back up and running." Ever had these words blasted over the P.A.? Ever seen the panic it induces? No doubt, teachers can and do teach with high performance even without technology. But in the modern world, performance can take a hit if technology doesn't allow connectivity or Wi-Fi to transfer performance into the world around us.

We value technology to connect to the outside world—to learn, to transmit, to bond. High-quality teaching also requires connection. And this means authentic, positive human relationships. Cynicism (often called *depersonalization*) is the third dimension of burnout (Maslach & Leiter, 2000). It involves negativity and pessimism, particularly involving people. Education is a highly social endeavor. When relationships are strained or cultures are toxic, the whole system suffers. Like Wi-Fi, teachers *can* teach without strong connections, but motivation and performance are diminished.

Throughout this book, we will be exploring ways to strengthen the performance of our teams beyond self-care. We will look at dozens of research-based strategies for strengthening our hardware, streamlining our software, and solidifying our connectivity. But next, we must acknowledge that even high-performing computers can crash.

The Crash: Unsafe, Unsecure Conditions

If you've ever experienced a computer crashing in the middle of a job, you know how devastating it can be. Memory is lost, programs need to be reloaded, and the system itself might require a massive reboot or new hardware. While computer crashes can happen without warning, we reduce their odds by analyzing and updating our system regularly. We ensure that the condition of the computer is set up for success. For educators, this means creating working conditions that provide safety and security.

From a neuroscientific lens, safety and security are critical to high-performance education. On a basic level, our amygdala, a part of the limbic system, helps us analyze external and internal stimuli for potential threats. And it's doing this all the time—some predict that our brain is processing up to 20 megabytes of information each second, but we only consciously attend to around 120 bytes each second (Bellis, 2015). So, in the background of our mind, our amygdala is deciding whether to trigger the sympathetic nervous system, often called the fight, flight, or freeze response.

Why does this matter? If teachers don't have a clear sense of safety and security, we get a double whammy hit to our performance. First, an educator's amygdala will be far more likely to trigger fighting, avoiding, or freezing up at work (ever seen this in a staff meeting before?). Second, when activity in the amygdala increases, activity in the frontal lobe—the house of rational, critical thinking—reduces (Goleman, 2006). We'll explore this more in Chapter 3 about stress and emotional exhaustion, but for now, recognize this: We don't get peak intellectual performance from people when they feel unsafe and unsecure. This means we can't ignore the two risk factors that put educators at higher odds of burnout: physical and psychological safety.

Physical and Psychological Safety

The years 2019 through 2021 swung us through some wicked whiplash. We flipped from the threat of active shooters rifling our schools to COVID-19 wafting into our lungs, all in the context of a social justice reckoning that was decades in the making. We switched from the daily tally of school shootings to virus death tolls climbing into the hundreds of thousands. One minute we are the frontline heroes scrambling to educate kids on Zoom. The next minute we are societal pariahs for wanting transparent procedures and policies to protect ourselves and our families from COVID-19. I went from walking into school wondering if I might be shot by a student to wondering if I might bring home a life-threatening virus to my newborn daughter.

One can argue about the low likelihood of a school shooting or a severe COVID-19 outbreak, but feeling unsafe at school is far from uncommon. One study found that 80 percent of teachers have felt victimized at school in the last year, and 44 percent reported being physically attacked (Mcmahon et al., 2014). Even the *potential* of being unsafe at school can shift our cognition to survival mode, wearing away at our sense of well-being (O'Brennan et al., 2017). If I'm often thinking about the threat of harm, I'm not dedicating my full mental faculties to high-rigor teaching, management, and engagement. And it won't be long before I start thinking of switching to other work that has far less threat to my safety.

One of the most important areas where school leaders can ensure safety for staff, then, is preventing and responding to intense student behavior. Students screaming in the face of their teachers. Throwing chairs and destroying classrooms. Physically assaulting staff. As schools look for ways to minimize suspensions, detentions, and traditional behavior approaches, sometimes the pendulum swings too far in the other direction—putting the onus back on the teacher to deal with behaviors that are both psychologically and physically unsafe. If we want educators to be at their best—and at work—we must take physical threats and events seriously and protect our staff. Ensuring physical safety for staff should be a proactive priority, and we should address threats to safety thoroughly and immediately.

We also must consider psychological unsafety, which isn't just the fear of physical safety: It is the sense of support, security, and inclusiveness. Thus, we can't ignore the disparity of psychological safety that exists for teachers of color. For example, although in the last few decades, hiring rates of teachers of color have increased faster than those of white teachers, teachers of color are leaving at faster rates (Carr, 2022). Nearly half of Black teachers reported they were likely to leave their jobs—twice as many as white teachers (Dileberti & Schwartz, 2021).

We speak often about the stress of teaching amid COVID-19, but how often do we consider the added stress of working in jobs that don't support diversity, equity, and inclusion? For many teachers of color, working conditions cause more than just stress—they create a lack of psychological safety and support. In their report "If You Listen, We Will Stay: Why Teachers of Color Leave and How to Disrupt Teacher Turnover" (Dixon et al., 2019), researchers cited five major challenges that are disproportionately affecting teachers of color:

1. They experience an antagonistic work culture that leaves them feeling unwelcome and/or invisible.
2. They feel undervalued, taking on more than their fair share of responsibility but are not recognized or compensated for their work.

3. They feel deprived of agency and autonomy to tailor teaching to the population of students they serve.
4. Their working conditions lack the supports needed for them to grow as professionals.
5. They bear the high cost of being a teacher of color, which takes a toll on them financially and psychologically.

Helping educators feel safe, supported, and included is critical for *every* staff member, but it is particularly critical for groups that historically (and continually) deal with systemic and societal prejudice.

Though we have so far discussed the topic of safety and security *at* work, we can't talk about retention without the topic of security *outside* of work. "In it for the outcomes, not the income" makes for a cute T-shirt idea, but it ignores a reality of retention: When income is low, workers will go. Our next risk factor of crashing is the topic of money.

The Elephant in the Room: Pay

"Salary. That's the number one reason I'm leaving." My friend and colleague Nick quipped this without hesitation when I asked him to describe his top reasons for leaving the classroom. "I realized that every year I had to put major life goals on hold, like buying a house or raising a family—and I was fortunate to come in without loan debt." Nick's decision to leave is a devastating one, beyond it being the exit of a friend. He was a highly effective teacher, adored by staff and students alike. He was involved in the community, creative, competent, and hardworking. He also had so much of what the research—and this book—admonishes: autonomy via teaching electives, relatedness via positive social connections with colleagues and kids, and competence and confidence via skill and humility.

The certainty of his answer, "pay," is a note of caution that strengthening organizational hygiene—like pay and policies—must be a priority. Psychologist Frederick Herzberg, a pioneer in the study of workplace conditions and employee motivation, identified that the factors that create motivation are *separate* from the factors that cause dissatisfaction (Herzberg, 1964). In Herzberg's study, 69 percent of the factors leading to dissatisfaction were what he called "hygiene" issues like low salary, micromanagement, and lack of security. Conversely, 81 percent of the factors leading to satisfaction were motivators like autonomy, recognition, and efficacy. We have to reduce the causes of dissatisfaction and increase the causes of satisfaction. As a case study, Nick had satisfaction: achievement, autonomy, affirmation, and advancement. But subpar policies like low salary and limited security create dissatisfaction, which were enough for Nick to leave.

This might explain why pay is one of the top considerations for whether a teacher stays or goes. One meta-analysis found that salary had the third-strongest association with teacher retention, trailing teachers' self-reported commitment to the profession and self-reported job satisfaction. Although the same study found that the top three reasons a teacher stays in the profession are positive student relationships, positive collegiate relationships, and secure employment, secure salary ranked fourth (Gundlach, 2022).

The importance of pay and benefits makes sense when we think about our hierarchy of needs. Pay represents security for ourselves and our family. Healthcare represents peace of mind that our physical safety can be supported. Pensions—which many states have slashed— and retirement benefits allow educators to work despite lower wages and more stressful conditions—to sacrifice in the short term for long-term security.

So why isn't this book all about pay? First, although pay is a top factor for teacher attrition, it isn't *always* the top; stress, for example, ranked higher on causes of teacher attrition according to a survey in March 2020 (Dileberti & Schwartz, 2021). Beyond the fact that pay isn't the *only* factor and isn't even always the top reason, the reality is that many school leaders have limited, if any, control over finances. Districts can't always influence what per-pupil funding is from state legislation. They might not have had a say in pensions getting slashed. Principals don't always control salaries, benefits, and bonuses. Not to mention that, state by state and district by district, there are major disparities in educator pay and cost of living.

But, while I can't predict the extent to which you have personal agency over educator pay and benefits, I can say that, collectively, we should work toward creating economic conditions that make educators feel safe and supported in this profession. Pay isn't the only way we fight burnout and attrition (see Figure 1.2), and job security involves more than salary and benefits. However, without respectable salary and benefits, the fight is much, much harder. Because, for every

FIGURE 1.2

Beyond the Salary Scales: Ideas for Strategic Funding

If adding to base salaries and benefits isn't viable, consider other ways to use finances to support retention.

1. **Early-career bonuses.** With college costs higher than ever, many early-career educators have no choice but to leave if their salary can't cover their basic needs. And the schools with the highest initial pay scale often win the best candidates.
2. **Mentoring and coaching.** High-quality coaching and mentoring, as we'll see in Chapter 9, is one of the greatest investments we can make to reduce burnout and increase retention. Don't treat mentoring programs as a box to check: develop, support, and fund them like your retention depends on it. Because it often does.
3. **Curriculum work.** Many educators have masterful skill in developing curriculum. Many districts shell out hundreds of thousands of dollars on packaged curriculum. Some schools don't pay staff at all to write curriculum—or only pay a fraction of what teachers can make developing high-quality curriculum for private companies. Investing in staff-generated curriculum is a win-win. Schools get high-quality curriculum relevant to their needs, and educators get the financial support they deserve.
4. **Tuition reimbursement.** Any support here helps educators—and the district. Investing in the continuing education of staff demonstrates a commitment to honoring their abilities and valuing their contributions. Studies of multiple reimbursement and retention bonuses found that direct payment to teachers, ranging from $500 to $5,000 bonuses, reduced attrition by 17–25 percent (Katz, 2018).
5. **Microcredentialing bonuses.** Another challenge of education is limited paths of career growth, beyond becoming an administrator. Open paths where teachers can gain specialized skills, opportunities to contribute those skills to the district, and financial incentives to do so. Create tracks that support district initiatives (e.g., SEL specialist, cross-curricular literacy coach, community coordinator, etc.).

teacher who stays despite the pay, there are talented educators like Nick who leave for greater economic security.

The Six Viruses

Some of the challenges of safety and security are uniquely flavored for education. My engineering friends, for example, aren't doing active shooter drills or working second jobs to afford their kids' college. But there are burnout causes that are characteristic across occupations. If we see the symptoms of exhaustion, cynicism, and inefficacy in our staff, we should look to these common causes: the Six Viruses of burnout. Chapters 3, 6, and 8 will explore these in depth, but for now, be aware that the prevalence of these can drain educator performance and increase the likelihood of a crash.

Chapter 3: Viruses of Exhaustion

1. Work overload
2. Lack of autonomy

Chapter 6: Viruses of Cynicism

3. Lack of fairness
4. Values mismatch
5. Lack of community

Chapter 8: Virus of Inefficacy

6. Lack of recognition

We can't mistake the symptoms for the cause of burnout. We see the strain, the struggle, the cynicism *in* teachers and then mistakenly place the onus *on* teachers to fix it. But it's the context, not individual character, causing educators to burn out across the world.

For the sake of our schools—for the sake of my wife—let's put our energy into creating conditions that allow educators to be at their best, so they can give their best to students who desperately need them.

If you're ready to download Educator Well-Being 2.0 into your school system, there are some critical mindsets and best practices that will upgrade your impact—and your school's performance—to a different level. It's time to explore the Illuminating Mindsets.

2

Illuminating Mindsets

Let's play a game of two truths and an untruth. You know the game? Someone shares three statements, and you learn which is true ("You *do* have a mutant 11th toe?") and which is false ("You don't actually love data meetings?!").

I was chatting with a school leader in a rural district of Idaho about staff well-being. As I was gathering information to understand what support the school needed, the leader said, "There isn't anything I can do. Teaching is just stressful. Our staff has to find a way to deal with the stress."

To be clear, the leader's tone was not one of resignation or heart-less disregard for staff well-being. She clearly *wanted* to help her staff (or she probably wouldn't have asked me to work with them). She just didn't know how. And, having worked with dozens of schools and hundreds of school leaders over the last year alone, I have heard these words, in different flavors, over and over again.

So which of the three sentences that she spoke is true and which is not? Let's start with the easy one.

1. "Teaching is just stressful." True.

Subjectively, teaching is very stressful. Three out of four teachers said that their work was often or always stressful. And the pandemic made it worse, with teachers listing "stress" twice as often as insufficient pay as a reason for quitting (Dileberti & Schwartz, 2021). Objectively, we could also agree that there are inherent stresses with education. We are attempting to provide individualized, equitable, rigorous education to a diverse population with limited time and resources. We care to do it well. And anytime we care deeply about an outcome, there will be stress. So yes, teaching *is* stressful. But is the next statement true?

2. "Our staff has to find a way to deal with the stress." True.

This one is a bit trickier. Should it be the educator's sole responsibility to deal with stress? No. But is it usually? Yes. As we're already seeing in this book, stress and burnout are caused by contexts and conditions, not a weakness of character. However, the truth is that an individual *is* the person left responsible for managing stressors—fair or not, in healthy ways or not. Maslach and Leiter (2000), our gurus of burnout research, captured this best by suggesting that educators often burn out because they are the "shock absorbers" of an organization—they must cope with the downward pressure and stress from administrative decisions *and* the upward pressures of managing student behavior and learning. On a technicality, then, the statement "Our staff has to find a way to deal with stress" is true.

3. "There isn't anything I can do." False.

Here is our untruth. One of the biggest myths a school leader can believe is that, because teaching *is* stressful and society is changing and challenging, there is nothing we can do but tighten up our bootstraps, take burnout on the chin, and charge forward. Societal and school stress is like the weather—we can't control it, but we can adapt to and prepare for it. And a school leader is one of the greatest sources of support in adapting and preparing for the stressors beyond a teacher's control.

Too often, school leaders underestimate how much influence they have over the well-being of their staff. For example, the quality of a school administrator is often cited as a greater reason for staying (or going) than salary. Attrition rates are more than twice as high for staff who strongly disagree that their administrator supports them and communicates clearly (Sutcher et al., 2016). On the positive side, leadership can be a major bolster to staff retention and well-being. For example:

Employees who feel

- Supported by administration are 70 percent less likely to burn out;
- Listened to by a manager are 62 percent less likely to burn out;
- Autonomous in approaching tasks are 43 percent less likely to burn out;
- Able to use strengths are 57 percent less likely to burn out (Gallup, 2020).

Not only, then, is the belief that "there's nothing I can do" a false statement—it may be the opposite. School leaders may be the *most* important factor in helping educators overcome the stressors and struggles of this critical work. If you're a school leader, you're no doubt used to "putting out fires" in the form of crises, but I'm inviting you to flip the metaphor and see yourself as the tender of fires, the person who helps others reignite and sustain their passion and purpose for education. Your actions can stifle the flames of your staff faster, or you can fuel a spark that illuminates a better present and future for students.

If you've ever tended or started a real fire (on purpose), you know that taking time and care to structure the fire can be critical to whether it burns or not. Rush the foundation, and you'll waste time trying to reignite it over and over. So too is the process of creating empowering cultures for staff. Rush or skip the foundation, and you may take more time or, worse yet, do damage to the process.

Before diving into the strategies of our Affectiveness Continuums, we need to lay the foundation—internally and externally—for illuminating better conditions and performance for school teams. I'm inviting you to adopt four mindsets that are key to the deep, important work of improving culture. Along with each mindset is an action step that, if followed sequentially, will illuminate a brighter path for you and your staff to improve well-being and performance.

Mindset #1: The Compass Mindset

Educators are masters of finding problems. Whether it's grammatical errors, missed steps on equations, or gum chewing in class, we make a living out of looking for deficiencies and intervening. But our knack for "not there yet" has a downside: we develop a habit of only seeing problems. A process that serves a purpose becomes our perspective on everything. From a psychological standpoint, this can lead to cognitive distortions: negativity bias (noticing and remembering the bad) mixed with inattentional blindness (focusing on one thing and becoming oblivious to others) combined with confirmation bias (focusing on details that confirm our predictions and ignoring evidence against it). The result? We focus only on fixing problems rather than optimizing opportunities.

I see this all the time when I speak to school leaders about burn-out. Their minds make a beeline for the problems and issues with improving staff culture. More often than not, for example, school leaders frame all their ideas for improved culture around the most cynical, burned-out person on staff—the hangnail of their hand, the person who, when offered free ice cream, complains there is no choco-late. Then, all the leader sees are the problems and roadblocks. The gripes at a staff meeting. The ways in which this staff member is "too far gone."

Anticipating challenges can be a productive *part* of the process. But, in considering this one hurdle of the hangnail worker, we some-times run into two more:

- We ignore the 98 percent of *other* staff who could benefit from new solutions and strategies.
- We get stuck on what we *don't* want rather than what we *do*.

Leaders, then, either give up on the goal ("So-and-so is just going to complain anyway") or set avoidant goals ("We need to address people being so cynical at staff meetings"). Avoidant goals, which are aimed at reducing the bad, or what *not* to do, are less effective than uplifting goals, which are aimed at desired outcomes, conditions, and actions. Compared to uplifting goals, avoidant goals lead to a lower likelihood of success, less positive relationships, and worse psychological outcomes (Elliot & Sheldon, 1998; Emmons, 1999; King & Emmons, 1991).

On the other hand (the one without the hangnail), there's evidence to support looking at increasing the positive rather than solely reducing the negative—a whole field called positive psychology. In actively cultivating the good, we not only reduce negative experiences but build resilience and greater coping for future challenges (Garland et al., 2010; Tugade et al., 2004). Training individuals to emphasize strengths leads to better work engagement and increased efficacy and resilience (Bakker & van Wingerden, 2020). Put plainly (and supported by meta-analyses): emphasizing and actively cultivating more of the good not only increases desirable work outcomes but also *reduces* undesirable outcomes (Donaldson et al., 2019).

A masterful navigator, then, doesn't ignore the thorny paths—they are very much aware of them. But they don't let the thickets define their journey. They know the importance of a Compass Mindset: establishing a clear, positive image of the destination and setting the goal *first* to avoid getting distracted on the journey (see Figure 2.1).

The last key idea here is to consider not just the value of the goals but also the systems that lead to them. As habit expert James Clear notes, "You don't rise to the level of your goals. You fall to the level of your systems" (Clear, 2018). What systems will increase the likelihood of these positively framed habits, traits, and behaviors?

For example, if you made the goal shift from "having people complain less" to "having workers adopt problem-solving approaches at staff meetings," what systems of communication would support this? Does it look like prepping staff for changes *before* meetings and prompting them to come with two concerns and three potential solutions? Does it look like ensuring meetings have ample, structured time and modeling for staff to work through problem-solving frameworks? Does it look like pulling select staff in for focus group conversations *before* presenting new plans and ideas to the whole staff? We don't rise to the level of our goals. We fall to the level of our systems.

With the Compass Mindset set, now it's time to explore the landscape to avoid bitter traps and ascertain better trails.

FIGURE 2.1

The Compass Mindset Action Step

Before establishing a plan, spend time reflecting on what positive traits, experiences, and habits are the end goal.

- What strengths of your school or group do you want to put to better use?
- What positive behaviors do you want when your staff is all together?
- How do you want people to *feel* when they come to work?
- How would you know staff would feel this way? What actions would they show?
- When presented with a challenge, what behaviors or mindsets do you want your staff to adopt?

To make this process even more impactful, invite other stakeholders into the process. Consider asking for input from a select group of students, parents, and teachers. Be sure to include teachers of all different levels and experiences.

Well-being and performance are just as much, if not more, about the *presence of good* and not just the *absence of bad*. As Maslach and Leiter (2000) write, "[T]he best way to prevent burnout is to promote engagement with work. It is not simply a matter of reducing the negatives in the workplace; it is also an attempt to increase the positives" (p. 77). Processing these questions will give you the end in mind as you explore the next mindsets.

Mindset #2: The Curiosity Mindset

Imagine this scene: A math teacher goes a whole year without providing a formative assessment—never attempts to gauge current skill or growth. Sure, the teacher occasionally sees a kid do some mental math. And the teacher tries out a cool math lesson they found online but doesn't link the lesson to any core skill and doesn't really pay attention to whether these lessons made any impact. At the end of the year, the teacher gives a summative assessment, although by the time the results are in, the students are no longer in class. When results are bad, the teacher wonders, "Why didn't students perform better?" Not the most effective way to improve math skills with students, right?

Now replay this scene, substituting "teacher" with "school leader." Swap "math skills" with "teacher well-being" and "math lessons" with "team-building exercise." This is how many schools treat teacher well-being and school culture. Leaders often don't collect—formally or consistently—data and feedback on well-being and culture. Sure, they might hear from a few staff members about issues. They might see that teachers look stressed and then google "team-building exercises" for a staff meeting. But rarely is feedback based on any measurable standards, nor is it used to make strategic changes to working conditions and support.

One backward practice that exemplifies this approach to staff culture is the exit interview. To be fair, it's not exclusively a backward practice in schools; many organizations and businesses use them as well. A person, having already decided to leave an organization, finally gets a chance to share why they no longer want to work there.

Exit interviews aren't backward because they invite feedback; they are backward because they ask for honest feedback *after* a transgression. The information can be useful for *other* people still in the organization. But that's like giving your ex feedback that helps their future relationships rather than open communication that could have saved *your* relationship.

For that reason, I'm a proponent of *retention* interviews rather than exit interviews. Imagine if, frequently, school workers were asked openly, honestly, and confidentially to provide feedback on how the school can improve working conditions, support, and strength building. Picture the potential for change if survey and interview questions were consistent and tracked over time. And what would it look like if school leaders took that feedback—nondefensively—and worked toward real solutions with the people who could benefit from them now?

If we want to create high-performance cultures and support staff well-being, we need to adopt a Curiosity Mindset: seeking genuine, frequent feedback about working conditions and motivation (see Figure 2.2).

Putting a Curiosity Mindset into practice might be the single most important practice in this book. First, as mentioned earlier, creating systems that allow workers to feel supported and heard could make staff less likely to burn out, 70 percent and 62 percent less likely,

FIGURE 2.2

The Curiosity Mindset Action Step

1. **Decide what data** you want to collect. Here are some categories worth exploring:

Dimensions of Burnout	Potential Causes	Motivators
• Exhaustion • Cynicism • Inefficacy	• Workload • Lack of autonomy • Lack of recognition • Value mismatch • Lack of community • Lack of fairness	• Autonomy • Relatedness • Competence

2. **Explore if surveys already exist**—work smarter, not harder—particularly those like the Maslach Burnout Inventory (MBI) or Areas of Worklife Survey (AWS) that have been vetted for decades.
3. **Establish who and when data will be collected and reviewed.** Review the data at least three times a year to ensure feedback is timely and action steps can be taken sooner than later (I recommend to the schools I work with to review the data after the first month of school, at the midway point, and 2–3 months before the end of the year).
4. **Communicate openly.** Share with staff what the data shows.
5. **Collaborate on action steps.** Invite staff into the process of developing action steps, strategies, and suggestions. While there might be a *lot* of suggestions, focus on one or two key areas at a time.
6. **Follow up.** Continue reviewing data, collecting new rounds, and having collaborative conversations with staff to work toward solutions.

respectively. Second, getting quality feedback as a leader takes the guesswork out of staff needs, creates a culture of collaboration and respect, and provides more creative solutions.

The most powerful way to implement a Curiosity Mindset is to treat it like academic data: Use standardized instruments and inventories so that reliable, valid data can be collected, reviewed frequently, used strategically, and compared across groups and times. Thankfully, you don't have to work hard to create these instruments; they already exist. The Maslach Burnout Inventory (MBI) is considered the go-to survey for gauging the exhaustion, cynicism, and inefficacy of a group or individual. Maslach and Leiter (2000) also developed an Areas of Worklife Survey (AWS) to look at what we call the Six Viruses. Together, these measures can help school leaders see the extent of burnout and the most likely causes that could be addressed.

Jennifer Moss, author of *The Burnout Epidemic* (2021), describes other useful questions, such as the following:

1. What is one change that would instantly allow you to be healthier at work?
2. How likely are you to feel satisfied in your job in 3 months (0–100; highly unlikely to highly likely)? (p. 149)

The first question gives qualitative feedback that can be immediately actionable for a school leader. For example, our district found a trend in 2021 when we asked this question. One of the most cited requests was to not be asked to sub on planning periods—a domino effect that led to greater exhaustion. Rather than just a vague number of how overworked our teachers were, we got insight on a specific cause that could be addressed by hiring more building subs.

The second question gives data on long-term projections of optimism or pessimism—and a sense of whether burnout is acute or chronic. Questions like this can reveal long-term predictions of dissatisfaction, which will require more in-depth long-term fixes. For example, one district I worked with asked the question "Where do you see yourself in regard to your career in the next one to three years?" Only 46 percent of staff stated they saw themselves still in the classroom as a teacher. The others anticipated leaving the profession (25 percent), retiring (20 percent), or shifting to a different role in education (9 percent). This data sparked in-depth changes such as increasing salary scales, reducing initiative fatigue, and strengthening support roles like mentors and instructional coaching. If we know the extent of the issue, we know the extent of the investment.

One key reminder is that, like academic data, we must be vigilant with developing high-quality questions. Moss goes as far as suggesting organizations don't DIY their questions—use valid and reliable surveys like the MBI and the AWS instead. Knowing that many schools might not have the budget to hire outside consultants to administer surveys, at the very least do your due diligence to collect quality data. Use the survey in Appendix A as a starting point.

In addition to having high-quality qualitative and quantitative data on staff well-being, it is critical that school leaders *show,* with clear actions, how the data is being used. Asking for feedback, and then doing nothing with that feedback, is a surefire way to create survey fatigue and ensure staff doesn't take feedback (or school leaders) seriously. To avoid this trap, be sure to utilize the next two mindsets.

Mindset #3: The Compassion Mindset

My love of frequent, actionable feedback stems from my experience as a teacher. In my early years of teaching, I adopted the preferred feedback model of academia: the end-of-semester survey. You know, the one where the professor leaves after the exam, students bubble in some feedback forms, put the forms in a folder, and then a random kid wanders campus like Frodo trying to figure out where to deliver the One Folder to Rule Them All.

Using this model, I ran into the same frustration I felt as a student. The feedback felt too little, too late. Often, students would give me feedback that would have been extremely helpful to know while they were still in class. So, in a precursor to the Curiosity Mindset, I switched my strategy to "Feedback Friday." Each Friday, students would respond to a quick question of "What is one thing I can do to teach you better next week?" Being amassed with so much honest feedback forever changed my teaching for the better. Just as valuable, I learned that I struggled with a major obstacle of growth: defensiveness.

If you've seen a teenager in their natural habitat, you know that *tact* isn't always on an adolescent's radar. While a lot of the feedback was affirming, some of it hit hard—especially if it was a critique of something I thought I was doing well. I've found similar defensiveness creep up when I request feedback on the workshops and PD I lead (and I've also learned that teachers can be even less tactful than teenagers).

No doubt, as you adopt a Curiosity Mindset and invite more feedback, you too will feel defensiveness creep up. To combat defensiveness and continue working toward collaborative solutions, the next step is to employ a Compassion Mindset: engaging empathy and actively looking for collaborative solutions to solve problems.

Now that I've brought up words like *compassion* and *empathy*, let's address the two ends of the continuum I often find school leaders on.

Continuum End 1: Empathy is touchy-feely, hippy-dippy talk.

This viewpoint—that empathy is a weak, sappy practice that lets others walk all over us—reveals a lack of understanding about what empathy is and why it's critical to leadership skills.

First, leaders already practice empathy all the time. There are three types of empathy:

1. Cognitive: anticipating what someone is thinking
2. Affective: anticipating what someone is feeling
3. Compassionate: helping resolve or reduce someone's struggle

I'd like you to try to imagine a day when you haven't used *any* of these skills to be an effective leader. Struggling to think of one? Probably.

No doubt the last time you had a difficult parent meeting, you applied all three. You had to meet with a parent to discuss concerning behaviors with their child. You knew that the parent might think their kid was being singled out (cognitive empathy) and that they might feel defensive (affective empathy). So, you thought of ways to help them see this meeting as solution oriented—mentioning all the supports in place, describing the student's strengths, offering the parent a chance to share what has worked for them at home (compassionate empathy). Whether it's a meeting with a parent, planning PD, or running a staff meeting, empathy is needed all the time, without singing campfire songs and crying into tissues (hopefully).

Empathy is necessary in virtually everything you do as a leader. So doing it well makes you a better leader (McKee, 2016). With this established, though, sometimes people swing too far to the other end of the continuum.

Continuum End 2: I don't need to plan my empathy—I'm a master.

On the other end, sometimes leaders (and many other people) assume that, because most of us innately use empathy most of the time, there's no need to hone it or apply it like a skill. "I'm an educator, so I'm a born empath," the logic goes.

But the further removed we are from a person's experience, the more we are liable to fall into empathy gaps—a diminished sense of what a person is experiencing, feeling, or needing. Educators are susceptible to this, despite any innate skills for empathy. Teachers, for example, gain more and more skill in an area, but their students' age and experience recycle each year. In particular, the more differences we have between ourselves and other people, the more likely we are to struggle with *affective* empathy (Silani et al., 2013). And, if we are in a high-stress state (as many educators and school leaders are), our ability to empathize with others is further impaired (Li et al., 2017; Suttie, 2017).

We have to consider empathy a skill like any skill we teach in schools. Some of us might find it easier to do than others, but everyone benefits from practice. And empathy *can* be improved with practice (Miller, n.d.).

So, I'm guessing that, because you are reading this book, you want to understand what your team is thinking and feeling and you want to reduce their struggle so they are more effective at work. And, if you'll be soliciting feedback to know these thoughts, feelings, and needs better, you're going to break down defensive walls to fully understand your staff. Therefore, it's worth investing in a Compassion Mindset (see Figure 2.3).

Mindset #4: The Creativity Mindset

Imagine you enter a room for PD and are told by a trainer to divide eight in half. *Easy*, you think. "Four. Can I get back to answering all my emails now?"

"How else?" the trainer says.

What does that mean? Half of eight is four . . . how much are we paying this trainer? He can't even divide.

But this isn't just any knucklehead trainer. This is distinguished Harvard psychologist Robert Epstein, PhD, considered one of the leading experts on innovation and creativity. This question of halving eight, beautiful in its simple trickery, is one of many empirically tested

FIGURE 2.3

The Compassion Mindset Action Step

Compassion and empathy are skills that can be applied to any situation—particularly as you get feedback from your staff on their burnout and need for better support. Here's what I call the 4 Ls:

1. **Listen nonjudgmentally.**

   By adopting a Curiosity Mindset and asking for feedback on staff well-being, you're already on your way to doing this. As you begin to hear what your staff's experience and needs are, it's key to think like a scientist: Consider the data from an objective lens, as though you are an unbiased researcher. Refrain from commenting, critiquing, or countering what others share as their experience. Instead, prompt them to share more. (My favorite follow-up line is "Tell me more.")

2. **Label the experienced emotion.**

   Emotion is tied to everything we do, especially when we are sharing experiences with burnout, motivation, and engagement. One misstep we often make is when we detach the qualitative data from the quantitative—looking only at numbers and disregarding the value of emotion as information. Every emotion serves a purpose; therefore, emotions are critical to understanding the needs and values of our staff. Here's a quick chart to look at three common emotions around burnout and what they might be attempting to communicate:

Emotion Family	Common Actions	Likely Causes	Needs Communicated
Anger (annoyance, frustration, exasperation, bitterness, fury)	• Attacking • Raising volume • Aggressive tone • Passive aggression	Being blocked in our progress via • Unfairness • Lack of control • Failure	Protection, boundaries, safety
Fear (trepidation, nervousness, anxiety, desperation, terror)	• Avoiding • Freezing • Hesitating • Withdrawing • Attacking	Perceived physical or emotional threat toward • Me • My community • My family	Safety and security from threat

FIGURE 2.3

The Compassion Mindset Action Step (Continued)

Emotion Family	Common Actions	Likely Causes	Needs Communicated
Sadness (disappointment, discouragement, resignation, helplessness, hopelessness, despair)	• Slowing down • Isolating • Crying • Seeking comfort • Ruminating	Something was or is lost	Community, healing, time to process

3. **Link commonalities.**

   Emotions can be unifying because we have *all* felt them. Even if we haven't lived the exact experience of others, we can relate around the emotion. After identifying a potential emotion being communicated to you, consider commonalities around its causes and needs.

   For example, maybe you want to introduce a new initiative but get a lot of feedback that is angry, frustrated, or aggressive. You examine this feedback like a scientist—possibly asking for more details—and learn (or surmise) that staff feel a loss of control over their already limited time and are overwhelmed by task fatigue. They need clear boundaries for their time and a sense of autonomy. As a school leader, you can relate to (a) the need for boundaries so you can dedicate full energy into meaningful work and (b) frustration when your autonomy is restricted (*cough, cough*, state mandates and red tape). Rather than getting defensive and feeling like their anger is a personal attack, you realize that there are identifiable causes and potential solutions. No longer is it you versus them; it's a group working together to reduce common struggles and achieve common goals.

4. **Look for collaborative solutions.**

   Linking commonalities cues a culture of collective effort rather than competition. But compassionate empathy puts affective empathy into action. Here we ask: what steps or strategies, within our control, could reduce struggle or increase strength?

exercises that improve creativity and innovation. Exercises that, in one study, increased idea generation for Orange County employees by 55 percent in eight months, leading to $600,000 in new revenue and savings of nearly $3.5 million through innovative cost reductions (Novotney, 2022).

Epstein's research has shown a critical idea for innovation: Creativity is not an innate ability that we either have or don't. Creativity is a skill that can be taught, a habit that can be built (Epstein, 2011).

For example, with even simple prompting like "come up with three solutions," you'd realize there are *many* other ways to answer the trainer's invitation to "divide eight in half." For example, you can take the visual *8* and draw a line horizontally, creating two circles. Split it vertically, and you create two opposite-facing *3s*. You could write out the word *eight* and draw a vertical line through the *g* or horizontally through the whole thing. Further, you could consider that *eight*, spoken aloud, could be *ate* and start dicing that word in half. Your brain just needed permission to think divergently.

Let's accept a hard truth: the existing practices of supporting staff well-being aren't working well. If the current practices *were* working, then I wouldn't be writing this book—and you wouldn't be reading it. Therefore, if we want to improve the culture and conditions of education, we will need creative, innovative solutions. While innovating educational systems isn't as easy as, say, dividing eight in half, it will require similar habits and practices. It will require a Creativity Mindset: implementing processes and practices to generate collaborative, innovative, and practical solutions.

Epstein's (1999) research has revealed four competencies that can boost a Creativity Mindset:

1. Capturing: preserving ideas whenever they emerge—using practices like carrying a notepad, leaving voice memos, or noting ideas on our phones.
2. Challenging: seeking new challenges—pushing our minds and skills beyond a comfort zone.
3. Broadening: seeking different types of knowledge and experiences—reading books, consuming media, or conversing

with experts in fields and on topics that aren't clearly related to our occupations and interests.

4. Surrounding: changing physical and social environments—working around new people, new locations, or even new artifacts and decor.

But perhaps the most important practice that school leaders will need is to embrace challenge and failure. Epstein (1999) captures this when he writes:

> New ideas emerge when multiple repertoires of behavior compete and one of the simplest ways to get multiple behaviors going is through the resurgence of old behaviors that occurs when current behavior is ineffective. When you are locked in a room, for example, every behavior that has ever gotten you through a closed door becomes more probable: jiggling the doorknob, pounding on the door, kicking the door, shouting for help, and so on. From these various behaviors, new sequences or new blends emerge. Thus, learning to manage failure—and not to fear failure—is an important means of boosting creativity. (p. 7)

Don't make the mistake of thinking that creative problem solving is a free-for-all, where anyone can try anything. Instead, ensure *practical* creativity using the action step in Figure 2.4.

Teaching is stressful. Educators have to find a way to deal with the stress. But thankfully, there's a lot you can do as a school leader to help them not only survive but thrive. Breaking the paradigms of teaching culture and conditions—paradigms that are stifling the flame of educator purpose and perseverance—will require a strong compass and foundations of curiosity, compassion, and creativity (see Figure 2.5). Habituating and embodying these mindsets as a leader will help you stoke the fire inside your team and illuminate a new, empowering path of education.

With these mindsets queued up, we're going to get into the details of burnout: What are the dimensions? What are the causes? And most important, how do we move from distressed to empowered, disconnected to engaged, and defeated to efficacious?

FIGURE 2.4

The Creativity Mindset Action Step

As we've seen, creativity has underlying mechanisms that can be applied to novel situations. No matter what problem we are trying to address, we can adopt the Creative Problem-Solving Process, which embeds Epstein's (1999) four competencies of creativity.

In short, this process involves bouncing back and forth between stretching possibilities via divergent thinking (unrestricted generation of ideas) and constricting thought via convergent thinking (analyzing and selecting the best idea).

- **Step 1:** Assemble your team. Make this team diverse.
- **Step 2:** Clarify the main challenge. This should be well established using the Compass, Curiosity, and Compassion Mindsets.
- **Step 3**
  - Divergent: Brainstorm potential causes of the challenge.
  - Convergent: Narrow down the top cause to tackle first.
- **Step 4**
  - Divergent: Brainstorm possible solutions.
  - Convergent: Narrow down to the most effective solution.
- **Step 5**
  - Divergent: Brainstorm ways to implement (who, what, when, where).
  - Convergent: Narrow down your top implementation strategies.
- **Step 6**
  - Divergent: Brainstorm potential roadblocks.
  - Convergent: Narrow down your most likely roadblocks.
- **Step 7**
  - Divergent: Brainstorm backup strategies/adjustments to avoid roadblocks.
  - Convergent: Narrow down the timeline, action steps, and assignments.

To utilize these steps, you should adopt some rules based on divergent and convergent thinking:

FIGURE 2.4

The Creativity Mindset Action Step (Continued)

Rules of Divergent Thinking:

1. **Separate and independent:** When people are asked to separate and brainstorm on their own, they usually generate 50–100 percent more ideas than if they brainstorm with others (Epstein, 2011). Even if you say, "Brainstorm on your own," someone usually interjects and it turns to a group conversation. So, make it a rule and set a timer to ensure the brainstorm is truly independent.

2. **Any idea goes:** Fight the urge to critique, shoot down, or question an idea during this phase. *Anything* is possible during this phase, so write down everything. The Convergent phase is for reasoning and analyzing.

3. **Limitless quantity:** The goal is to produce a high quantity of ideas, so the only limit set should be a time limit for brainstorming. Build off ideas, combine them, list them without explanation—anything to produce as many options as possible.

Rules of Convergent Thinking:

1. **Continuums, not dichotomies:** Keep ideas—even crazy ones—on reserve in case elements of the idea could be useful. Rather than scrapping ideas as "good" or "bad," line them up on a continuum of most/least practical or most/least impact.

2. **Question ideas, not people:** Be civil in how you evaluate ideas. Also, be sure to hear explanations out fully—and ask good questions—rather than rejecting ideas straight away. Sometimes the details spring new ideas.

Creating better working conditions isn't easy work. Just as a flashlight doesn't clear trees, the Illuminating Mindsets don't guarantee a smooth, easy journey. But a lighted path is easier to navigate than fumbling in the dark. These mindsets are designed to build off one another to strengthen collaboration, generate effective solutions, and provide actionable feedback so that, no matter how thorny your path, you have a process for clearing the thickets.

As you work to embody these mindsets, consider them functioning like a cycle. Each round may reveal new insights that require fine-tuning goals and seeking information to generate more creative solutions.

FIGURE 2.5

Mindset Cycle

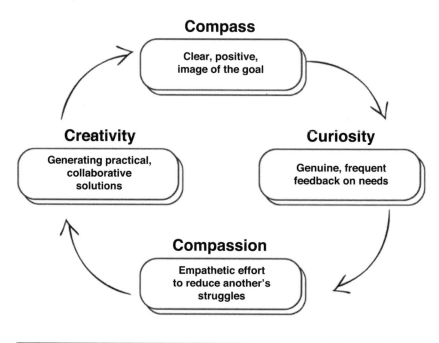

PART II

Distressed to Empowered

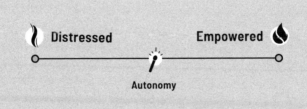

Distressed   Empowered

Autonomy

3
Emotional Exhaustion 101

Everyone has a "buffering" moment. You've seen your computer buffering—stalling—when trying to download something or run a critical program on a computer. But humans buffer too. Here's what that looks like: Once, you were unexpectedly called on to answer a question, say something, or do something. Maybe it was a cold call when you were a student. Maybe a curveball during an interview. Maybe a cranky parent screaming at you. Whatever it was, it *instantly* shot your stress levels up.

In a microsecond, your composure was rocked. You changed physically. Blood rushed to your face, increasing oxygen flow from your airways. Sweat ramped up as your body heat soared. You fidgeted or shifted as your arms and legs prepared to fight, fly, or freeze. You might not remember these physical changes, but you surely remember a cognitive one: you didn't answer to your best ability.

Maybe your mind locked up and you sat in frantic silence ("Uh . . ."). Maybe you started gushing out illogical thoughts, circling around whatever gibberish was spilling from your mouth ("What I meant to say was . . ."). Whatever you said, it probably wasn't how you would have responded under calmer circumstances (though you've rehearsed for years what you *should* have said). You might not even remember the facts of the moment, recalling, instead, the emotions (e.g., embarrassed, angry, scared). We've all buffered. And buffering reminds us of a key idea:

Stress affects performance.

How we think and behave is a direct extension of how we *feel*. If you can understand how a short-term buffer affects performance, imagine the effects of an extended buffer. How many educators have been buffering for weeks, months, or *years*? How much student learning is lagging because a teacher's skills aren't streaming at 100 percent?

Let's explore the effects of emotional exhaustion, one of the three critical dimensions of burnout. How does emotional exhaustion affect performance? Why does it happen? And most importantly, how do we create cultures and contexts that reduce buffering and increase our capacity to stream our best work?

Stress: The Good, the Bad, the Ugly

Here's an exercise to try. Pause reading and go get a glass and some water. No, seriously—go get some water. Burnout aside, you probably need to drink more water.

OK, here's how it's going to work: We're going to pour water into the glass to understand the good, the bad, and the ugly about stress and emotional exhaustion (see Figure 3.1). The water in the glass will represent our stress levels at any given moment. The space left in the glass will represent our capacity to think logically—to be calm, cool, and collected, or "stream" our abilities without buffering.

Now pour a little bit of water into the glass. Key insight number one: our glass is never empty. We *always* have stress in our system. Most people have heard of distress. But not often do we hear about *eustress*, which is healthy and helpful stress. Stress can cue three critical responses for our survival:

Rise Response: An athlete seems to defy gravity in a game-winning play. A musician loses sense of time, becoming "one" with the audience. A parent anticipates a child about to fall and swoops in to help. These are examples of the challenge or *"rise"* response. The rise response (a) narrows our focus, (b) increases our energy, and (c) helps our body divert resources to take action.

FIGURE 3.1

The Cup of Stress

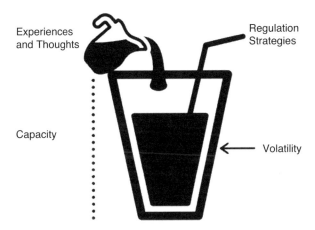

Experiences and Thoughts

Regulation Strategies

Capacity

Volatility

Stress is incredibly complex. Many factors affect our stress levels: the ratio of hormones like cortisol and DHEA, the memories we associate with an experience, our genetic disposition, or even our mood at the moment of a stressor.

Generally, we have a particular threshold of stress tolerance or *capacity* (often associated with *allostatic load*). To some extent this is influenced by our genetics, although our experiences can influence how our genetics express themselves. Prolonged raising or lowering of our normal capacity can create a "new normal." Sometimes this is good, such as with exercise. Other times this can be detrimental, such as with chronic stress beyond our control.

How quickly we move from eustress (healthy levels of stress that *enhance* our performance) to distress (unhealthy levels of stress that *inhibit* performance) is our *volatility* (McGonigal, 2016). Trauma, for example, can make a person more likely to be emotionally hijacked, even to innocuous experiences. Conversely, confronting stressors in a safe, supportive environment can make us more stress resilient (less volatile).

Both our capacity and volatility can also be influenced by our regulation strategies. Consider: What are all the different strategies you use to manage your stress? And, to what extent do you match the right strategy to the right situation? In Appendix D, you can learn the D-Stress Strategies—the five categories of stress management that every person should know and use.

Reflect Response: You have memories that you may never forget—days and specific moments that have defined who you are. These memories are vivid because they are usually saturated by intense emotion—pleasant or unpleasant. When your body experiences stress, it releases a flood of hormones to strengthen your memories and increase your neural plasticity. The opportunity for us, though, is to not let reflection turn into rumination.

Reach Out Response: Many believe that humans became the highest species because we prioritized individual "winner-take-all" mentalities. This is far from the truth. Humans survived against stronger, faster, and more ferocious foes because of our ability to form tribes. Even our facial expressions, for example, are theorized to alert others of our needs. Stress often channels us to "tend and befriend" by helping us seek support, help one another, and empathize with others. Stress isn't always a cue that something is wrong—it often means we need help to make something right.

Now, before you downshift and say, "Mwahaha! Stop whining people! Stressful conditions are good!" realize that the benefits of stress exist when it is acute (temporary) and within our control (we have autonomy in reducing it). So please don't smack a colleague and claim it's a eustress exercise (even if you really want to).

But let's get back to our analogy. As we go about our day, these stress levels increase or decrease depending on several factors: external events, circadian rhythms, dietary decisions, and our internal thinking. Let's watch this play out in the typical day of an educator.

You've just woken up for your day. Pour more water in the glass. Our stress levels are naturally boosted when we first wake up. Why? Because our brains evolved to be on high alert after arising from the vulnerable position of sleep. We're wired to be on instant defense against threats, whether they are saber-toothed tigers or screeching alarm clocks.

Add some more water. Why? Because you're probably sleep deprived—as 35 percent of adults are (CDC, 2016). When we limit our physical resources, our brains double down on preparing for survival via the stress response.

What do most adults do when they are sleep deprived? Chug caffeine. Add some more water to the glass because the by-product of that espresso-induced alertness is increased stress levels. So, it's 6:12 in the morning and we haven't even started *functioning* yet. Then this thing called life happens.

You think about all the upcoming stressors of your day—disgruntled parent meetings. Angsty students. That overly chipper colleague. Add some water to the glass. You scramble to get yourself—and your family members—out the door. You forget to pack your lunch, you can't find your keys, and somehow Billy Junior lost his sock *even though I just gave you your socks! How'd you lose them?!* Add more water.

You hop in your car at the *precise* minute necessary to make it to work on time only to find that every other driver is driving wrong—too fast, too slow—doesn't matter, *they're all wrong!* Add some water. You peel into the parking lot only to find that *someone has parked in my parking space!* Sure, it's not marked, *but they should know that's my spot!* Add some water nearly to the top.

You scramble into the halls of your school, lockers slamming, kids screaming, early birds ready for chipper-chatting. Then someone taps your shoulder for attention, and you reel around yelling, *"What?!"*

You've snapped. Because, if you look at your glass, you'll notice there's not a whole lot of room left for logical thinking or empathy or equanimity. Your brain is sloshing for survival. Psychologists call this emotional hijacking (Goleman, 2006). When activity is high in our amygdala, the emotional processing part of the brain, activity decreases in our prefrontal cortex, a major part of our executive control. Put simply, there's an inverse relationship between unpleasant emotional arousal and rational decision making.

Occasional high levels of stress can happen, and acute moments of high stress aren't necessarily a bad thing. But, when these rises become chronic, day after day, week after week, this becomes emotional exhaustion. And so many of us are walking around *all day* with these high levels—our cups of stress filled to the brim. And it is the chronic exhaustion that is eroding educator well-being and performance.

The Devastation of Exhaustion

Emotional exhaustion is the canary in the coal mine when it comes to burnout. Almost always, our burnout *starts* with exhaustion (Maslach & Leiter, 2000; Moss, 2021). Increased emotional exhaustion also causes increased cynicism and inefficacy. And the effects of emotional exhaustion are pervasive, not only wearing down the educator but also eroding the culture and success of the school.

Let's start with the most important devastation of exhaustion: students do worse in school when teachers are exhausted. A large-scale assessment study found that teacher exhaustion had a significant, negative correlation with student achievement in mathematics, even after controlling for teacher experience and student demographics (Klusmann et al., 2016). Another study involving 380 teachers and 7,899 students determined that teacher exhaustion not only negatively affected standardized test scores but also diminished class grades, school satisfaction, and perception of teacher support (Arens & Morin, 2016). Students with exhausted teachers are also significantly more likely to get referrals and in-school suspensions (Eddy et al., 2020).

Stressed and exhausted teachers can't give their best because they aren't at their best. But that's assuming they stay in the profession. There's the whole quitting education thing too, with "time pressure via emotional stress and exhaustion" one of the main reasons teachers leave the profession (Skaalvik & Skaalvik, 2016). For those that stay, exhaustion has huge implications: highly stressed teachers have worse job satisfaction, higher absenteeism, lower engagement, and lower efficacy (Greenberg et al., 2016). One can see the downward spiral: High stress and exhaustion lead to lower performance and less people— which means workloads get shifted onto those who stay, further exhausting them.

The bottom line is that stress and exhaustion reduce performance. And if we care about performance, we need to reduce the stress and exhaustion. But what are the biggest causes?

The Viruses of Exhaustion

"One More Thing?": Work Overload

"I can't be asked to do one *more* thing." I heard this, in exasperated tones, from colleagues after our student-support team recommended a new initiative. What was the huge ask—the massive time request of the initiative? Informally trying to mentor one student. That was it.

One student. Teachers received a list of students who had several at-risk factors. And the support team asked, "If you could casually try to build a connection with one of these students, it could make a big difference on their success in school." In a twist of irony, this initiative—increasing positive relationships with students—could *reduce* emotional exhaustion (Taxer et al., 2019). But many teachers resisted.

How could an educator reject such a basic idea—connecting with one new kid? Surely, they must be heartless curmudgeons who feast on the souls of children? Not at all. These are compassionate and hard-working colleagues who *love* kids. The rejection of a new initiative—no matter how small—is a symptom of a *context* flaw, not a *character* flaw. Their minds couldn't handle the addition of more tasks.

The leading virus of exhaustion is excessive workload (Maslach & Leiter, 2000). It's death by 1,000 cuts. One small task gets added to dozens, if not hundreds, of other demands competing for our energy and resources. The demands *within* the classroom are exhausting enough. Education articles often suggest that teachers make thousands of decisions each day—decisions about more than how to scarf down a lunch in 20 minutes. But it's not only the fatigue of high-level teaching. It's the *additional* tasks, requests, and responsibilities. Research has found that "[t]he most common professional work context challenge was lack of time due to heavy workloads and non-teaching duties such as paperwork or meetings" (Beltman et al., 2011, p. 190).

According to a 2019 Gallup poll, those who say they strongly agree to having too much work to do are 2.2 times more likely to burn out (Gallup, 2020). For some educators, excessive workload is a particular threat. Multiple surveys show that teachers work an average of 13 hours a week of overtime (National Center for Education Statistics, 2003; Bill and Melinda Gates Foundation, 2012). Remember that cup of stress analogy? When Swedish researchers studied stress hormone levels in workers, they found that those who work more than 10 hours a week of overtime had cortisol levels twice as high as those who don't (Moss, 2021). That's right—many teachers might have *double* the stress in their cup than if they could complete their work within their contracted hours. On the flip side, those who say they do have enough time to get work done are 70 percent less likely to experience burnout (Gallup, 2020).

We have a dilemma, then, when considering workload: There are *infinite* things we could get done in schools, but there are *finite* hours in the day. Unfortunately, when the pressure mounts to get work done, some school leaders engage a counterproductive practice: micromanaging staff. This brings us to our next virus of exhaustion.

Snakes Eating Themselves: Lack of Autonomy

The Ouroboros is an ancient symbol, depicting a snake or dragon eating its own tail. The Ouroboros traditionally symbolizes the eternal life cycle: birth, death, rebirth. Unlike many ancient symbols, though, a snake eating itself *is* a rare but real thing. Also, unlike the beautiful symbolism of Ouroboros, the real event in nature is not so pretty.

You can find videos online of snakes eating themselves, though I don't recommend it, especially if you dislike snakes as much as I do. I'll spare you the twisted visuals (pun intended) and tell you what happens: Because snakes require external conditions to manage their body temperature, sometimes they get overheated. Overheat can lead to disorientation and a false sense of hunger as metabolism speeds up. This wicked combo can lead to a snake mistaking its own tail for prey. The snake latches onto its own tail and starts digesting—a process that is difficult for a snake to stop on its own. Unless someone changes the environment (e.g., the environment cools or a veterinarian intervenes), the snake kills itself (American Tarantula & Animals, 2022).

While a snake eating itself in nature is very rare, the process happens all the time in schools. Here's what it looks like:

We've seen already that educators at all levels experience excessive workloads, which leads to greater burnout and less productivity. As performance dips, pressure picks up—affecting students, teachers, and school leaders. This high-pressure "body heat" of the school gets out of control, leading us to target the character of our own staff (the snake's tail) rather than the context of the working conditions (the real threat). So, we lash out with a self-sabotaging action called micromanagement. We think that controlling, dictating, and demanding more will force educators to step up. We replace trust and guided autonomy with scripted curriculum and reduced choices. This only adds to the pressure, exhaustion, and burnout. And the cycle continues.

Gross snake-eating-itself analogy aside, there's real data on the devastating effects of tightening control on workers. Micromanagement is associated with lower morale, higher turnover, and reduced productivity (Rogers et al., 2021). Those who experience burnout are three times as likely to feel micromanaged—and it's concerning here that 63 percent of educators felt micromanaged in the last week (Collins & Collins, 2002). Micromanagement can also be a two-hit punch to the gut: (a) talented teachers reject micromanagement to opt for different jobs or careers and (b) micromanaging policies erode autonomy, reducing personal responsibility for one's work (Hargreaves, 2003).

It is imperative that we break the cycle of exhaustion and pressure that creates distressed and burned-out educators. But now you are probably thinking, "So what's a school leader supposed to do? *Never* ask teachers to do anything? Let schools become a free-for-all of siestas and fiestas?" While school siestas would be amazing and I'll take any excuse for more fiestas in my life, reducing educator exhaustion doesn't require coddling conditions or work-when-you-want chaos.

Let's pour out a little of the "What am I supposed to do?" stress in your cup and explore how to reduce exhaustion while *increasing* performance, well-being, and school culture. Let's talk about reducing workload and increasing autonomy.

4
Reducing Workloads

Nellie Leary was probably freezing the morning she arrived for work on a March morning in Massachusetts. Compared to the wet, near-freezing air outside, the sheltered wood walls of the Grover Shoe Factory offered a probable promise of warmth. Though it's hard to find exact records, Nellie was probably still a teenager, as many factory workers were in 1905. The work of shoemaking was taxing, despite the advances in sewing machinery, but Nellie probably knew that at least she had some income and at most she had a safe way to spend her days.

But stitching together "probablies" still leaves seams of "possiblies"—seams that can burst when the pressures of life build.

When David Rockwell lit the boiler to heat up the Grover Shoe Factory on the morning of March 20, 1905, he did so reluctantly. Not because he didn't want the shift workers to be warm on the frigid morning, but because he was forced to use the 14-year-old boiler instead of the newer model, the latter requiring a routine mainte-nance flush.

Nevertheless, the boiler had done its job just fine the past 14 years, even as the factory grew new floors and wings. So, when Rockwell stepped out of the factory that day, he did so with the belief that things would probably be safe.

However, pressure doesn't abide by "probably." Despite the history of security, the boiler stirred and strained, steam building and packing below the four factory floors. The plant manager, noticing a "peculiar humming" coming from the radiators along the north wall, attempted to call Rockwell. But he had already stepped out of the factory.

Five minutes later, the pressure became too much for the steel seams. As the boiler exploded with the force of 300 kilos of dynamite, it tore from its stanchions, rocketing through the four floors, killing several workers, and setting the factory on fire.

Nellie Leary probably didn't think that would be her last day. Nor would she have predicted that she would be among 58 coworkers who lost their lives in the Grover Shoe Factory Disaster. And she wouldn't have known that her fate would prompt massive reforms and regulations to industrial safety that still continue today.

Reading bulletins from the National Board of Boiler and Pressure Vessel Inspectors is not something I do on the regular. I didn't even know there was a National Board of Boiler and Pressure Vessel Inspectors (or that they released semiannual publications).

But the concept of "building pressure" piqued my curiosity after speaking with a superintendent about the concept of work stress. We spoke at length about the perception of work—how it seems like previous generations saw work as work and how he had never known a time when his coworkers or staff haven't felt overworked.

What this conversation revealed—confirmed, when juxtaposed with countless similar discussions with other school leaders—is that many of us fall into a false dichotomy: work is either stressful or it's not. The variation of this belief is that, when workers suggest reducing workload and stress, they are seeking a profession of paradise, punching a clock for heavy wages and light lifting. Either work is work—suck it up and accept it—or "do what you love and you'll never work a day in your life."

But emotional exhaustion is not a dichotomy. And identifying a need for relief is not a cry for margaritas in Cabo. Instead, exhaustion and stress are like the pressure gauge of a boiler. The pressure is inevitable and a part of a well-functioning system. But, if allowed to build without mechanisms to release it—especially if systems aren't secure and well-maintained—the pressure will burst to disastrous ends.

The tragedy of the Grover Shoc Factory, while extreme, demonstrates the danger of relying on old systems, not monitoring pressure levels, and not releasing pressure before it reaches devastating extremes—whether we're talking steam or stress.

In our last chapter, we identified the dangers of emotional exhaustion for workers. And we identified the two viruses—work overload and lack of autonomy—that most contribute to chronic stress. In this chapter we will look at how school leaders can "release the pressures" of work overload in ways that increase the efficiency, energy, and effectiveness of school staff.

Reduced Workload: The More Efficient System

The Big Three

Time is a finite resource. One would think that, with all the advances of technology, we would have found plenty of ways to do more in less time. Unfortunately, this isn't the case, especially because emotional exhaustion is a subjective experience. The median number of hours teachers teach each week is 54. For teachers *unlikely* to leave the profession, their median work hours were 52, while those *very* likely to leave, that hour was 57—meaning just a few more hours of work each week can take its toll on intentions to stay.

This is particularly problematic for Black teachers. "Black teachers report spending more time working (65 hours per week as compared to 53 for white teachers and 48 for Hispanic teachers) and less time teaching (20 hours a week) than either white or Hispanic teachers (25 hours a week)" (Education Week, 2022, 20).

Of the hours spent in a typical work week, the median amount of time *actually* teaching was only 25. Other areas continue to push pressure on an educator's schedule:

1. Grading/feedback (3–5 hours)
2. Planning/prepping lessons (5–6 hours)
3. PD and meeting with colleagues (2–3 hours)
4. Administrative, school committees, and extra duty tasks (5–6 hours)

No rational educator would eliminate these things entirely. Lessons have to be planned. Students need feedback. Data needs to inform our decision making. But here we have a clear application of our pressure gauge analogy: We reduce workload by helping educators minimize the pressure while being more efficient in these areas. The most requested areas where teachers want *more* time are (a) teaching students and (b) planning and preparing lessons. So, teachers don't want less work; they want less work that gets in the way of teaching high-quality lessons.

Even the idea of *reducing* any of these areas yields pushback from many educators and school leaders—they are so embedded into how we have done school for decades. However, a massive, controlled study calls into question whether these practices we rely on might be a part of dated, inefficient systems—old boilers that aren't effective.

The United Kingdom's Department for Education recently organized a massive study across eight regions, involving dozens of schools, hundreds of educators, and nearly 11,000 students. Schools hosted controlled, longitudinal studies, testing a variety of practices to reduce workload and increase educator well-being—all while tracking effects on student performance. In total, the research team was able to do a meta-analysis of 112 effect sizes. They tested strategies like the following:

- Feedback practices
  - Flash grading (grading fewer student responses)
  - Peer grading
  - Whole-class verbal feedback
- Data monitoring
  - Reducing the frequency of data collection
- Lesson planning
  - Simplifying lesson planning sheets

Among the many surprises of these studies (e.g., a national department of education actively sought to *reduce* teacher workload and increase well-being?!), there are three that are most significant for our purposes (Churches, 2020):

1. Interventions reduced the average additional work time from 1 hour and 20 minutes per day to 30 minutes a day;

2. Reducing workload consistently boosted teacher well-being—decreasing feelings of workaholism and increasing self-efficacy, optimism, love of learning, and enthusiasm;

And, drum roll please!

3. Reducing the workload consistently had no effect or a *positive* effect on student performance.

That's right. At worst, decreasing workload had zero effect on student achievement. At best, students actually improved their performance when their teachers were less stressed and overworked and provided more specific, immediate feedback, spending more time learning as opposed to taking progress-monitoring tests. In other words, we don't reduce workloads to make educators feel warm and fuzzy inside; we reduce workloads so they have the space and capacity to teach more efficiently.

It's time we update our systems and reduce workload while also being more efficient and intentional. We need strategies to relieve the pressure of exhaustion.

Strategy #1: Establish a Zero-Sum Rule

Anyone who has written a curriculum for a class knows that you can't add a new lesson without reducing or cutting another. Sure, you can accelerate a lesson or condense it, but even this acknowledges that tasks, activities, and assessments need to be adjusted.

Unfortunately, we forget to apply this same principle—time is finite—to our initiatives. We add in a new process or program without first asking, "What are we going to cut or reduce in order to make time for this?" Often this happens implicitly; an administrator might know in their minds that they aren't going to worry about a previous process. But, without an explicit rationale and permission, many educators will continue putting themselves under pressure to do all the things that have been asked of them previously.

Start by implementing a "zero-sum rule" for any new task, process, or procedure. Before implementing a new idea, do a realistic assessment of (a) how much time it will take to learn or enact, (b) where this time is going to be freed up from existing tasks, and (c) how this shift will be clearly communicated to staff.

It's critical to engage Illuminating Mindsets here—especially Curiosity and Compassion Mindsets. Having a zero-sum rule presents some sticky considerations for a school leader. For example, some initiatives might be passion projects for certain staff members. Too much shifting and cutting can exacerbate cynicism and learned help-lessness if staff feel they are pinballing between initiatives. Be sure to get feedback from staff—whether whole staff or focus groups—to plan for adding and removing initiatives. In describing the reduction of initiative fatigue, superintendent and author P. J. Caposey writes, "The thing that stuck out to me is the emotional toll it takes on teach-ers when initiatives they helped introduce or promote just fall by the wayside. . . . Listen to your people" (Caposey, 2022, paras. 13, 14). In the next strategies, we'll cover how to make a zero-sum rule effective while reducing the "pinballing" of constant change.

Strategy #2: De-implement Initiatives

Forty. That is the number of initiatives we recognized that our small rural district has attempted in the last few years. As a part of our school improvement process, we spent a few minutes listing out every initiative that has been started—to varying degrees of continuity and success—in just a few years. Figure 4.1 is the sample (get your "educa-tion acronym" bingo sheets ready!).

Numbers are relative, and some districts might have double or triple that amount; however, 40 represents an average of 7 initiatives per building in a few short years—6 being the *maximum* number of initiatives any school should adopt at a time, according to some initia-tive fatigue experts (Reeves, 2011). Some of these initiatives are minor, hovering in the background. Others involve hours, weeks, or years of full implementation—curriculum sets, PD days, meetings, meetings, and more meetings.

What we learned through the process of "initiative inventory" was how many programs and processes our educators are juggling in

FIGURE 4.1

List of Initiatives

- Capturing Kids Hearts
- CHAMPS
- PBIS
- Explicit instruction
- Trauma-informed practices
- Zones of regulation
- Cognitive coaching
- Instructional coaching
- Flex Academy
- San Francisco Math
- F&P Classroom K–5
- Amplify
- LMS: Buzz
- Open Up Resources Math

- School Messenger
- Google Classroom
- Accellus
- Exact Path/Edmentum
- Google Classroom
- Seesaw
- PLCs
- Quantum Learning
- NGSS/MSS
- AP curriculum: PC
- RTI process
- PLUS TIME
- MTSS tiered instruction
- ELL support (SIOP)
- Lifeguard mentoring

- Mentoring with BBBS
- Study hall
- Autonomous PD track
- Smart boards
- STAR character
- SEL committee
- MICIP process committee
- HUMANeX Culture Development
- CCSS alignment
- Chromebook integration
- ALICE training

the air, not to mention this whole COVID-19 thing that rocked *every* process and program to its core. One elementary educator I know has *four* new curriculum initiatives implemented this year alone—four pacing guides to review, four scripted lessons to learn and sequence. When the teacher's principal mentioned they were looking into adding a new SEL curriculum, I can imagine a collective ulcer emerged in every teacher's gut. Even the most talented and experienced teacher can burst at the seams (like a boiler) when too much initiative pressure builds up.

Every school leader should be asking, "Are we doing too many things with mediocrity rather than a few things with excellence?" In *Leading with Focus*, Mike Schmoker (2016) urges leaders to "simplify: to severely reduce the focus of our efforts so that we can take the time necessary to clarify, train, retrain, practice, repractice, monitor. . . . Effective leaders protect their teachers from an unfocused array of professional development offerings" (pp. 88–89). You, the school leader, are the greatest release valve of workload pressure. Release regularly before the overload creates irreparable damage.

Initiative overload becomes initiative fatigue for many reasons. First, it leads to cynicism ("Why bother? In two years we'll move onto some new buzzword in education"). Like a punch to the gut, switching to new initiatives sucks out our energy as we feel all our effort was for nothing. Second, we have diminishing returns—most initiatives aren't deeply integrated because we are spinning too many plates in the air. And third, adding another initiative exacerbates empathy gaps. We forget that even a "small ask" gets piled on top of countless others that were asked first. What seems urgent and important to us is often one of many "urgent and important" asks an educator or school leader is already responding to. And that's before we talk about major initiatives like new curricula.

Therefore, we must learn to *de-implement initiatives*. There are three ways to do so:

1. Reduction or partial reversal.
2. Substitution with something related.
3. Discontinuation or complete reversal.

Here's an example using weekly assessments to progress monitor literacy:

1. **Reduction or partial reversal:** We are going to use monthly progress-monitoring assessments instead of weekly; monthly will still provide plenty of data and more time to make use of the information.
2. **Substitution with something related:** Our current assessments are too cumbersome to administer and track. We're going to use a shorter, faster version instead.
3. **Discontinuation or complete reversal:** Progress-monitoring assessments aren't adding anything we don't already know from existing formative assessments. Eliminate them.

Similar to the *zero-sum rules*, when de-implementing any initiative, activate a Curiosity Mindset and ask for feedback or input from staff (and, I would argue, before *implementing* one as well).

Ask your staff questions like the following:

- What is one initiative that, if it were off your plate, would help you do your job better?
- What elements of [the initiative] should we keep that allow us to [goal of the initiative]?
- Are there elements of [the initiative] that we should scrap while still being able to achieve [goal of the initiative]?
- Are there things we already do that already provide [goal of the initiative]?

There's a larger reason why we should look to reduce initiatives: Too often, initiatives are just fancy, cumbersome, and expensive versions of what educators know is best practice anyway. Programs don't change performance. Practices do.

Strategy #3: Value Practices over Programs

In his book *Finding Your Leadership Focus*, Douglas Reeves (2011) writes, "If you want to begin to challenge initiative fatigue in your school, you must start with a widespread recognition that we must focus on practices, not programs, to gain deep implementation" (p. 10).

I've seen and experienced this far too many times: A program gets brought in to fix a problem when all we needed was support and time to strengthen existing practices. How many different "character development" programs have we seen—different packaging with the same ingredients, hours and hours of preparing for the launch, only for it to fizzle because the promises of the program didn't coach and support real change in teaching practices?

Before jumping into the program that promises educational paradise, reflect on whether supporting key practices might be a better, cheaper, and more empowering use of time. Value practices over programs. Use the following questions as prompts (and notice how they engage Illuminating Mindsets):

- What is the desired outcome?
- What three to five practices would we see as evidence of implementation?
- What do staff members gain by implementing these practices?

- What roadblocks might stall the habituation of these practices?
- How will we support the implementation of these practices?

When you are identifying desired outcomes, go deeper than an increase in test scores. For example, although "boosting verbal scores on the SAT" may be an end goal, focus on the instructional practices that you would see in classrooms that would produce this end goal. You might identify that students having rich, text-based conversations would create the critical thinking needed to boost verbal scores. With this in mind, the practices you hope to see might involve things like referencing direct quotations to support arguments, making inferences based on textual evidence, discussing rhetorical choices based on an author's purpose, and more. These practices can be strengthened *without* adopting a new, bright, shiny, expensive curriculum set.

Rather than pedantic PLC conversations around the minutiae of CCSS.RI.11-12.6 showing up on SAT questions 3, 18, 19, and 25, staff can be empowered with time, permission, and support to troubleshoot strategies for analyzing rhetorical choices in the texts they are already using. They can look *ahead* rather than *back*.

Rather than spending thousands of dollars to hire a consultant to spend whole days training a new curriculum, you might realize that your teachers simply need opportunities to watch each other pilot these strategies, provide each other feedback, and share resources. With reduced workloads and increased time and support, internal resources make external resources obsolete.

Strategy #4: Midcourse Correction

As an extension of placing practices over programs, evaluate what has stalled your existing initiatives. Before adding something new, perform a *midcourse correction*: troubleshooting how to better support existing work taking place in an area of need. In "Making Change Last," Eric Beaudan (2006) suggests some of the following prompts when change stalls:

- **Resistance:** "Who is opposing the change and why?"
- **Focus:** "Which other initiatives or priorities are diverting our attention from completing this change?"

- **Energy:** "How can we renew people's enthusiasm for change?"
- **Casualties:** "What are the unexpected side effects the change caused? How can we acknowledge and minimize these?"
- **ROI:** "What performance improvements can we really attribute to this change?"
- **Communication:** "How do we share what we've learned and ask for feedback and inputs from people?"
- **Sustainability:** "How can we make sure the changes we're introducing will become institutionalized?"

Another strategy for midcourse correction is to take a group of staff and have them *separately* use the prompts for a specific initiative. Then, come together and see if you have alignment. You might quickly realize that even within your team you have different views of the desired outcome of the initiative. You might differ wildly on what are the three to five core practices you would expect to see. Therefore, a midcourse correction might be a more appropriate use of time and resources than investing in a whole new initiative.

Strategy #5: Revamping Data Meetings

One of many traditions we cling to is the data meeting. Every month— or even every week—teachers meet to review progress monitoring data and discuss ways to improve instructional practices. It's a great practice in theory. Teachers collaborate, stepping away from the silos of their classrooms and have deep, intentional conversations about shifting core teaching practices. Right? But there's one problem: data meetings might not work.

Heather Hill, of the Harvard Graduate School of Education, analyzed 10 studies on the impact of data meeting practices. Across the 10 different programs, Hill found, "zero [showing] impacts of getting teachers to really be productive, understand what kids don't know, and change their instruction" (Geller, 2022).

As with most things in this beautiful world we call education, the issue isn't the theory of data meetings—it's the practice. Effective data teams are characterized by deeper-level thinking, such as analysis, synthesis, goal setting, and reflection. They move beyond external attributions for performance and focus on strategies. In reality, a data meeting looks more like this:

Teachers gather. Someone says, "I don't even need to look at the data to tell you what the problem is." A frustrated teacher vents about student motivation, limitations of standardized tests, full moon Fridays sending society into chaos. Someone quips, "We don't need more data—I already have more data than I know what to do with!" Affirming nods . . . yet the show of data must go on because tradition demands it. Many minutes of finding the right spreadsheet . . . then verifying the right spreadsheet . . . then realizing the spreadsheet is missing data . . . then adding in the data. Discussions commence over question 12, standard 12.5.8-b-201c. Detailed dialogues about how the options were *actually super confusing—no wonder they missed that.* A stoic agreement that the answer option will be changed for next year. Crickets chirp as no one volunteers. Narrowing in on the content of question 12, someone yawps, "I have an idea!" Passionate deliberations take place about an activity seen on Pinterest. A quest begins to find said Pinterest worksheet. Quest accomplished! More yawps! Passionate plans commence over the sharing of the holy grail of worksheets. The clock strikes 4 p. m., and the data show concludes. "Same time next week? Oh . . . forgot we have the staff meeting. Maybe next month."

Alright, this is a cynical, exaggerated look at data meetings (sort of). What this hyperbolic narrative identifies, though, is that data meetings are often ineffective because (a) we probably spent more time entering data into various spreadsheets than *discussing* data; (b) we get distracted by external attributions; (c) we rarely talk, learn, or explore changes to core teaching practices; and—most of all—(d) we are data abundant and time deficient.

Before the data defenders defenestrate this book, I'm not suggesting that we ignore data or not have collaborative conversations. Instead, I'm suggesting we be clearer and more intentional about the goal of a data meeting: to change instructional practices. If our goal is to have high-level conversations about teaching practices— and actually spending time changing those practices—a better use of time might be the *inter-* and *intra-coaching* strategies described in Chapter 9.

As every great athlete knows, you can only learn so much from reviewing game day footage. At a certain point you need to learn, practice, and implement new skills. Activate a Curiosity Mindset and ask your staff, "How can our data meetings better support learning, practicing, and implementing new skills?"

Strategy #6: Coach for More Efficient Feedback Systems

For years, the bane of my existence was evaluating high school ELA essays. One can only read so many *To Kill a Mockingbird* thematic analyses—can only see so many students mixing up Scout and Gem—before one's soul extinguishes. After reviewing 120 of these at a time, the little spirit I had left was crushed as students ignored my detailed feedback, flipping to the back page to see the grade, and throwing the papers in the trash bin (or on the floor). With each trashed essay, the hours and hours of my weekend floated down into Dante's seventh circle of teacher abyss.

But I found salvation in the doctrine "work smarter, not harder." I soon learned that pre-conferencing with students while they drafted led to more thorough revisions, better-written work, and more timely feedback. I learned that single-point rubrics gave students a clearer focus. I learned that a well-crafted rubric and student self- and peer reviews did most of the work for me. Most of all, I learned that efficient, timely feedback systems could reincarnate my lost grading hours into better student learning.

Studies by the U.K. Department for Education back this idea up. In the studies that explored more efficient grading systems, students performed just as well if not better than control groups. And students often felt more positive, supported, and successful. Best of all (for us frustrated ELA teachers), staff went from spending 5–10 hours a week grading to 2–4.

Unfortunately, most teachers are left to figure out these efficient strategies on their own, much as I did. Invest in saved time and sanity and coach for more efficient feedback systems, including

- **Flash grading:** focusing in on a select few problems or elements to evaluate and provide feedback.

- **Peer grading:** Utilizing in-class collaborations for students to give each other feedback.
- **Oral grading:** Effectively engaging students with verbal prompts to analyze their own work and notice and correct mistakes.
- **Conferencing:** Giving students targeted feedback in person, either individually or in groups.

Like an upgraded boiler system, coaching to develop more efficient feedback systems helps educators reduce workload pressure now and in the future.

Strategy #7: Stop Requiring Lesson Plan Submission

"Discouraged. Disillusioned. Distrusted." This was how Shelly reflected on being required each week to submit lesson plans to administration. "I never had clarity on what the goal or purpose was. Was it to prove we knew how to organize lessons? Was it a hoop to jump through to appease upper admin? Was it a tool to guide classroom instruction and clarity of student outcomes?"

Despite having previous teaching experience, each week Shelly had to detail seven things for each class section she taught, each day (objectives, standards, materials, resources, learning activities, etc.). "Everything just piled up. I would spend hours and hours of my time beyond contractual hours—at home, on the weekend, over school breaks—trying to fill out the forms. It negatively affected my life at home, my relationship with my administrator, and my sense of value from my school." Then there's this irony: "It took so much time just to complete the document that I didn't have time left to work on actually developing or improving quality lessons."

Shelly's experience—not uncommon to other teachers who are required to submit lesson plans—demonstrates two great casualties that often come from required lesson plan submission. First, teachers lose a sense of trust and value. Big Brother surveillance might not be the aim of this practice, but it's hard not to feel the dystopian distrust from your school leaders. In many ways, required lesson plans become a form of micromanagement, leading to both exhaustion *and* cynicism.

The second major impact is the workload. It takes a *lot* of time and energy to map out perfectly detailed lesson plans. Rather than focusing on developing new practices, improving feedback systems, or having collaborative coaching conversations, teachers must plug away at lesson plan forms—knowing full well that (a) the lesson may change anyway as they respond to student needs and (b) administrators probably aren't even looking at every detailed plan because they have their own workloads to manage. Lesson plan submission is yet another practice with a low return on investment. A lot of time goes into something that rarely changes instructional practices for the better.

Like so much of what we do in education, lesson plan submission often misses the target it intends to hit. It's a theory that, in practice, adds more burden than bolster to a teacher's work. Let's look at two goals of lesson plan submission and more worthwhile alternatives.

Goal #1: Consistent Educational Experience for Each Student

No student should have a subpar education because they have teacher A instead of teacher B. If lesson plan submission is meant to shore up inconsistencies, instead provide built-in time for co-planning.

Designate contractual time in your weekly schedule for teachers to co-plan. The goal here is not to make every teacher robotically replicate the same lesson (more on autonomy soon). The goal is to make sure that common learning targets are met. Teachers can share ideas, resources, and instructional practices during this time to not only hit learning targets as a team but also improve their instruction through collaboration and collective efficacy.

Goal #2: Sound Lesson Design Practices

Another common purpose of submitting lessons is to make sure that teachers are using sound lesson design practices, such as backward design, implementing formative assessments, using content-rich activities and resources, and more. Without coaching or reflective conversations, submitting weekly lesson plans doesn't ensure this is achieved. This is akin to having a basketball player run drills on their own without any coach to give them tips and feedback—maybe they naturally figure out new skills, or maybe they simply habituate bad ones. Instead, coach for effective lesson design practices.

Using the prompts for practices over programs, identify the practices you most want to see in a solid lesson. Focus on one at a time, providing training, coaching, and collaborative support to help teachers understand the what, why, and how of the practice.

For example, many school leaders insist on seeing objectives from lesson plans posted in classrooms at the start of a lesson. But I can tell you what most overworked educators do: They post generic objectives that can tick the boxes of evaluative walkthroughs, rarely using them to enhance instruction. Why? Because without explanation and experience with how stated objectives can improve student learning, there's little buy-in for this practice. Imagine if, instead of spending hours each month submitting lesson plans, teachers used this time to

- Learn the neuropsychological benefits of priming.
- Translate standards into relevant and strategic outcome statements for a unit or lesson.
- Develop outcome statements into formative assessment strategies.
- Create student self-reflection and peer-coaching methods using outcome statements.
- Infuse clear outcome practices into existing classroom opening and closing routines.

Doing a deep dive into changing a practice will provide greater buy-in and authentic improvements than surface-level lesson plan submission. As a teacher, the shift here is from doing something to tick boxes and pass an evaluation (submitting lesson plans) to doing something that benefits me and my students directly (time and support for improving a practice).

Whether lesson plan submission is a requirement of your school or not, ask yourself this: Are your teacher requirements providing Big Brother coaching or Big Brother compliance?

We take a lot for granted in our workdays. Our working conditions are miles ahead of factory work of the early 20th century. We don't have to worry about boilers bursting at the seams, shooting steam and fire through our halls and classrooms.

But that's because, when society recognizes physical dangers to the workforce, policies, procedures, and protections are put in place to increase safety. But the threats to our health and wellness are not just physical—they are psychological, social, and emotional. And although these are invisible threats, we've seen how they are very much real threats to our well-being (there's a reason the World Health Organization lists burnout in its International Classification of Diseases).

If we care about our staff as people, we must treat workload the way we treat boiler pressure—installing better systems, increasing efficiency, and most of all monitoring and releasing the pressure before it's too late. Nellie Learie deserved better conditions. Modern workers deserve the same, whether it's working boilers or sensible workloads.

5
Autonomy

Let's explore human motivations. What drives us to do what we do? And how can school leaders leverage motivation to boost staff well-being and performance? To explore motivation, here's a great discussion topic for your next leadership conference—one that will bring up the beautiful (and bizarre) effects of human motivation: What's the weirdest thing you've had to "investigate" as a school leader?

No doubt you struggle to choose from the *many* strange investigations over the years. Take, for example, our recent incident of the kid who drank formaldehyde from the science class pig cadaver. So many questions. Did he actually do it? And if so, why? How would we prove it? Was it a dare, and if so, should other kids be brought into the investigation? And what does one *do* with a formaldehyde chugger . . . detention? Free pass to the hospital? Restorative circle? (I'm really bummed the last one didn't happen.)

Things get weird in education, sometimes daily. So weird that we often think, "There's no other occupation that deals with this kind of craziness." But we live in a wonderful world brimming with weirdness because human motivations lead to all sorts of interesting behaviors, whether we are in education, medicine, finance, or even the hallowed halls of the legal system.

Guilty with a Chance of Meatballs

When Leahman Glenn Robert Potter walked away from the scene of the crime, his shirt was splattered with red stains. It wouldn't take a blood spatter analyst much time to assess what happened, as a smattering of red flecks of cooked flesh clung to his mouth and cheeks. There was no denying the crime. The victim didn't stand a chance.

Of course, the victim was a pot of meatballs, so, to be fair, it didn't stand a chance to begin with.

Picture the crime: The guy gets so hungry he walks into someone's garage, gorges on Grandma's meatballs, and absconds with tomato stains. The next thing he's under arrest, and dozens of human lives are pulled into hanger-induced drama.

Authorities must have had a "student chugged formaldehyde?" level of curiosity when they were called to the scene of the missing meatballs. They probably thought, "Are we really doing this?" as they questioned eyewitnesses about what they saw that day. The attorneys must have wondered what their profession had become as they considered whether to "negotiate away the unlawful taking charge. . . . Because the offense here consisted of nothing more than eating food and setting down the owner's pot" (Miller, 2008).

Why am I bringing up this story in a book about teacher well-being? Well first, for my own entertainment (reading the news bulletins and lawyer briefings was a hoot). Also, to point out that education isn't alone in dealing with the bizarre manifestations of human motivation. But more to our purpose, it highlights how

- All human actions—no matter how strange—are motivated by core needs; and
- Whether these needs are met dictates whether a person fights to survive or functions to thrive.

In this chapter, we are doing a deep dive into a core human need that shapes the motivations of educators: autonomy. We'll identify why it is so important to fulfill, how increasing autonomy reduces exhaustion, how the lack of autonomy erodes the profession, and most of all, how to fulfill this need to increase retention and performance.

But I hate to tell you: I'm not ready yet to move on from our dear friend the meatball bandit.

Unsatisfied Need: Unsatisfied Staff

Leahman was hungry. And his hunger became a legitimate defense in his trial—this concept, *"hangry,"* became a topic of medical study and legitimate research (Digestive Health Team, 2021). We've all been there (although, maybe not standing outside a stranger's house palming meat chunks)—so hungry that we aren't functioning at our best. Hunger is a stress state, and, in Chapter 3, we saw the effects of stress on our performance. Also, Ed 101 gave us a primer on Maslach's hierarchy of needs, suggesting if certain needs aren't met, a person struggles to thrive.

Simmering these ideas down (like a slow-cooker meatball) gives us the basic model illustrated in Figure 5.1.

FIGURE 5.1

Needs Flow Chart

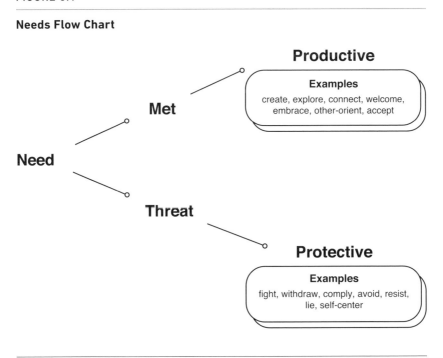

If a basic need is met, people have the cognitive and emotional capacity and the willingness to be productive. If, however, this need is threatened—even if we *think* it will be threatened—our behaviors become protective.

Look at the sample behaviors from people who are protective versus productive when their needs are met. Then, apply a Compass Mindset: Which behaviors am I striving for with my educators? Do I want them to fight and resist any change we need to implement? Do I want them doing tasks with low, self-centered effort just to comply? Or do I want a staff that can embrace change, meeting it with creativity, curiosity, and care for others? If you want the latter, then we have to meet the needs of our staff first.

This makes sense implicitly if we only think about physical needs. Imagine if, for example, you prohibited your staff from eating food or drinking water at work. No lunch breaks. No vending machines or snack baskets. No food. No drinking fountains. Depriving someone of their basic physical needs would create maligned behaviors such as noncompliance or rebellion.

However, Harvard psychologist Henry Murray suggests that people have needs of the mind just as they have needs of the body (Deci & Flaste, 1996). The needs of knowledge workers go beyond physical. We must treat autonomy—the need to feel aligned with one's choices, values, and interests (and the power to do so)—as equally critical to the productivity of our staff as we treat physical needs. Your staff might not be hungry for meatballs, but they are starving for autonomy.

The What of Autonomy

A central idea you may have noticed in this book is that we often think of things in dichotomies rather than continuums. We inaccurately think people are either always stressed or never stressed. We can fix everything or we are powerless to everything. But life is full of more continuums than dichotomies. Our latest example is what I call the False Autonomy/Chaos Dichotomy. The line of thinking is this: If I give people autonomy, they will do whatever they want, which will cause massive conflict, which turns into chaos, and therefore autonomy equals chaos.

But let's define autonomy: "endorsing one's actions at the highest level of reflection" (Deci & Flaste, 1996). Autonomy, then, is high when a person's behavior aligns with their values, interests, and needs. Ultimately, autonomy is having the ability to make choices in our lives and professions. "Choice is the key to self-determination and authenticity" (Deci & Flaste, 1996, p. 10). Here is where we can think of autonomy on a continuum.

Take curriculum, for example. A school may require that a teacher teach a canned, scripted curriculum—mandating exactly what, when, and how to teach. The teacher has little to no choice; therefore, autonomy will most likely be low (although it is still possible to be autonomous if the canned curriculum aligns with the teacher's values, interests, and needs). The option is not either (a) use the canned curriculum or (b) throw it out altogether. Within the curriculum, teachers could be given autonomy to choose better texts that align to their students' needs. They might have choices on *how* to pace the content in a way that ensures mastery of an outcome before moving on. They may have options for how to assess students and how to use that data.

Therefore, when we consider providing autonomy, we don't have either *control* or *chaos*. We have degrees to which educators have choices that allow them to align their behaviors with their values, interests, and needs.

If we mistakenly believe that autonomy is all-or-nothing, we can also fall into a trap on the other end and give no structure or support. Too *much* choice can be a bad thing. Without having the information, support, and skill necessary to make an informed choice, "being given a choice will feel more like a burden than a support for autonomy. It may well engender anxiety, and without adequate information, people are likely to make mistakes" (Deci & Flaste, 1996, p. 36). We want to avoid the extremes between no choice or too much choice.

The guiding questions we should ask as leaders are "Where can I offer my people more choices? And how can I make sure these choices are about things that truly matter to them?" The well-being and performance of your educators hinges upon autonomy.

The Why of Autonomy

In Chapter 3, we explored the negative effects of micromanagement—how adding pressure and reducing choices leads to lower morale, higher turnover, and reduced productivity. Perceived pressures at school also negatively affect teachers' sense of self-efficacy (Leroy et al., 2007).

However, controlling educators doesn't just erode their intrinsic motivation and performance; it trickles down to negatively affect learners. A highly controlled teacher becomes a highly *controlling* teacher as pressure passes from leader to teacher to student. Like rocks stacked on top of each other, the ones bearing the weight of the pressure are those at the bottom: students.

One study explored the effects of teachers being told, "Remember, it is your responsibility as a teacher to make sure your students perform up to high standards." Ever said something similar?

Compared to a control group, the "high standard pressure" teachers talked twice as much, made three times as many directives, and said three times as many controlling statements (Deci & Flaste, 1996). A study of school-based curriculum for elementary students showed similar issues. Teachers who faced external pressure toward higher standards similarly engaged in controlling behaviors in their classrooms. The pressured teachers were also less effective: their students showed poorer performance on objective test score outcomes (Flink et al., 1990).

Should we have high standards? Absolutely. But, as a leader, consider whether your drive for high standards is a boulder or a bolster. Does it support motivation or spur compliance? There's a difference between the command "Do (this) to have high standards" and the question "What support do you need to achieve high performance?" Adopting a Compassion Mindset means being mindful that top-down pressure creates a sense of control, which diminishes the very thing we seek to create: high-performing classrooms.

But there's good news. Supporting teacher autonomy yields the high performance we seek. For burnout, having a sense of choice is a critical element of having an internal locus of control—a belief that one can influence their own outcomes. Educators who have a sense of internal locus of control have lower burnout rates than those who adopt external locus of control mindsets (Judge & Bono, 2001). On the staff well-being and retention side, workers of autonomy-supportive managers are more trusting of the organization, less concerned about pay and benefits, and display higher levels of satisfaction and morale (Deci & Flaste, 1996). Educators who are encouraged to tap into autonomous motivation have decreased burnout and an increased sense of self-actualization (Roth et al., 2007). And remember how autonomy is a continuum and not a dichotomy? The more a teacher moved up the continuum of autonomous choices, the more they felt accomplished, withstood challenges of teaching, and reduced their burnout (the opposite was true as they moved *away* from feelings of autonomy).

More autonomy for teachers reduces the downward pressures affecting students. Teachers are more likely to be supportive of students' autonomy if they perceive their principals to support *their* autonomy. And the kids we serve are the greatest beneficiaries: Students of autonomy-supportive teachers are more curious and master-oriented, and they evidence higher self-esteem (Deci & Flaste, 1996). They also experience more positive emotions, are less distracted and anxious in class, give more prolonged effort, center their learning more on comprehension, get better grades, and are less likely to drop out (Pelletier & Sharp, 2009).

The benefits of autonomy support far outweigh efforts to increase control, which are detrimental to begin with. Ultimately, we are talking about increasing choices that allow educators to satisfy their natural drive to align their actions to core values and needs. We're providing choices that allow teachers to be at their best. Our Compass Mindset, then, is helping staff be more efficacious and intrinsically motivated through autonomy. Given that there are countless ways to support autonomy through choice, let's discuss where to start.

The How of Autonomy

"Where should we order out?" This question, a mirage of joyful anticipation, is more often a jolt of anxiety. There's a phenomenon in relationships known as the Paradox of Dinner Choice. Two individuals, tasked with a decision of where to dine out, must come to consensus. Ironically, the more options provided, the more overwhelming the choice. I painfully remember a day when my wife and I spent no less than 30 minutes debating where to eat. "Chipotle? No . . . we had tacos for lunch today. Pizza? Nah . . . last time I had that much dairy it destroyed my gut." After much googling, guessing the other's desires, and deliberating online menus, we finally settled on our go-to Chinese takeout spot . . . only to realize it was 8:03 p.m. They closed at 8:00. We ate cold sandwiches from the fridge that night, salted with our crestfallen tears.

The paradox of choice affects more than a dinner dilemma—it presents an overwhelming array of options for a school leader. Where is the best place to give teachers autonomy? From their research for *Trusting Teachers with School Success: What Happens When Teachers Call the Shots,* Farris-Berg and Dirkswager (2012) identified 15 areas where schools effectively build in autonomy—each area containing variations and degrees of autonomy, including

- Learning programs
- School-level policies
- Schedule
- Work hours
- Selecting colleagues
- Choosing school leaders
- Professional development
- Evaluating selves and colleagues
- Assessments—type, occurrence, weight, style
- Budget

Like a city of takeout restaurants, each option presents pros and cons. Where to begin? The easiest way to narrow these choices is to adopt Curiosity and Compassion Mindsets and survey staff needs for autonomy. As a starting point, you could ask staff, "In what area of your work do you wish you had more control?" This question can highlight major trends that inform your autonomy support.

However, like too many dinner options, this starting point may provide a lot of differences that muddy decision making. In that case,

I'd recommend borrowing a strategy my wife and I now use to make dinner choices: three options. Rather than asking, "What do you want for dinner?" one of us prompts the other, "Give me three options that sound good for dinner." The prompter then chooses one of the three, and we eat a delicious meal that isn't soggy with our tears.

In a school setting, given the endless array of autonomy options, the key is to focus on the areas that most directly affect a teacher's day-to-day needs, interests, and values. For that reason, I recommend we consider these three our top options:

- Learning programs and curricula.
- Professional development.
- Assessments and use of data.

Figure 5.2 offers what a more focused autonomy support survey could look like.

Strategy #1: Autonomy Support Survey

Modify the prompts depending on your school or needs. For example, secondary schools may consider the role of elective courses as an opportunity for curricular autonomy, whereas elementary schools may explore the choices a teacher makes about the daily scheduling of literacy and math and how to include sciences, social studies, and more.

It may seem ironic to restrict the choices available for autonomy support; however, as we've already mentioned, *too much* choice can increase anxiety and stress because people get overwhelmed with too many choices. Narrow it down to options in which we know teachers crave autonomy.

Upon getting feedback and direction from staff, now it's time to adopt the Creativity Mindset and look for ways to increase autonomy in the area you've prioritized. Every school's needs and approaches to autonomy support will look different. But here's my biggest piece of advice as you move into the Creativity Mindset phase: use the power of the pilot study.

FIGURE 5.2

Autonomy Support Survey

Rate your current perception around each of the following on a scale of 1–10
(1 = I'm overwhelmed with too many choices; 10 = I want more autonomy).
Consider how your current level of autonomy is impacting your ability to teach
effectively.

1. Learning programs and curricula

Daily lesson design	1	2	3	4	5	6	7	8	9	10
Pacing/sequencing	1	2	3	4	5	6	7	8	9	10
Text/resource choices	1	2	3	4	5	6	7	8	9	10

Please elaborate on how this is affecting your ability to teach effectively:

If you desire change, what might this look like?

2. Professional development

Choice of topic	1	2	3	4	5	6	7	8	9	10
How to implement	1	2	3	4	5	6	7	8	9	10

Please elaborate on how this is affecting your ability to teach effectively:

If you desire change, what might this look like?

3. Assessments and use of data

Choice of assessments	1	2	3	4	5	6	7	8	9	10
Use of data	1	2	3	4	5	6	7	8	9	10
Frequency of collection	1	2	3	4	5	6	7	8	9	10

Please elaborate on how this is affecting your ability to teach effectively:

If you desire change, what might this look like?

Strategy #2: Pilot Studies

Change is hard because it requires risk. We move from the known to the unknown. Even if individuals aren't content with their current conditions, the adage "better the devil you know than the devil you don't" lingers in many minds, preventing workers from trying new things. This is where pilot studies can be helpful.

A pilot study selects a group of individuals to enter an experimental condition while allowing others to stay in the control condition. In creating new approaches to autonomy support, using a pilot study is helpful for many reasons.

1. It allows individuals the choice to participate.

We support autonomy two-fold by allowing individuals to choose whether to try out a new approach. Conversely, for those who are anxious about change, overloaded with other work, or skeptical of the approach, they can let others do the experimenting first.

You might wonder, "What if no one or a small number of people wants to try this new approach?" Reduce this likelihood by ensuring that

- You've truly utilized the Curiosity and Compassion Mindsets to understand if this is an area where teachers really want more autonomy.
- You've clearly communicated the what, why, and how of the plan. Assemble a small committee to analyze the plan ahead of time to ensure it is well-designed and communicated.
- You've considered how the plan might shift workloads. Many people will opt out if it's more work, so make sure that either the workload isn't increased or—if it has to increase—that teachers are compensated for the increased workload or exempt from other workloads.

2. It helps work out implementation kinks.

Even if you do analyze your plan in advance, no doubt challenges will come up. A pilot allows you to test out issues and learn from mistakes before mainstreaming it for your staff. As you pilot a new approach, build in feedback checks to learn mid-process.

Additionally, the very nature of a pilot study allows us to compare our staff's experience to the control. We learn the pros and cons of the new approach compared to the status quo, thus making more informed decisions on how to proceed.

3. It creates grassroots movement.

Our biggest marketing asset is our staff. We can preach the value of a change for an entire staff meeting (please don't do this), but teachers will always look to their colleagues to see if it's *genuinely* worth their time. A pilot group, then, can advocate on your behalf, speaking to the experience, the benefits, and the tips for doing it well.

To illustrate what this could look like, Figure 5.3 is an example from a recent pilot I helped develop for my former school.

FIGURE 5.3

A Pilot Study Example: Autonomous Professional Development

Professional development is an essential area to support autonomy. According to one study, increasing teachers' reported influence over their professional development goals from *some* to *a lot* is associated with a nine-percentage-point increase in intention to stay in teaching (Worth & Van den Brande, 2020). It also allows educators to build efficacy in ways most valuable to them.

In the state of Michigan, schools are required to provide 30 hours of professional development. Typically, this involves administrators plotting out all 30 of those hours, deciding the learning focus for the whole staff. Here, we saw an opportunity to pilot autonomy. Because administration values common focus for PD, we didn't want to eliminate whole-group PD altogether. So, for all staff, 15 of the hours of PD were the same. However, for the remaining 15 hours, staff could opt into one of two groups:

- **Traditional Track PD:** 15 hours of PD decided by admin. Teachers would attend PD time the same way they did any other year. Fifty-one percent of our staff chose this option.
- **Autonomous Track PD:** 15 hours of PD focused on an area of interest that the teacher chose. Forty-nine percent of our staff chose this option.

FIGURE 5.3

A Pilot Study Example: Autonomous Professional Development (Continued)

The Autonomous Track developed "passion projects" that aligned with their values, interests, and needs. Working with an instructional coach (me, in this case), Autonomous Track teachers identified one area that could benefit their students, their colleagues, and/or the school culture. Then, they set a goal and a systematic plan for learning about the area and/or implementing new strategies. They could also team up together around shared goals. I checked in throughout the year with each teacher to get feedback on the process, help guide their thinking, and find support and resources as needed.

For the 15 hours, teachers had full choice of how to approach PD. They could visit other schools, attend webinars and conferences, do book studies, and more. They collected evidence of learning and tracked their time. Importantly, they were able to flex their time. For example, our district had the occasional half- or full-day PD time each month. During these PD days, Traditional Track teachers attended PD organized by the administration. However, an Autonomous Track teacher could go home early during this time, so long as they logged the three hours at a different time—either before or after.

The culmination of the project was the symposium at the end of the year. During the final half-day, Autonomous Track teachers shared their projects with the whole school in workshop-style presentations. Traditional Track teachers could choose which of their colleagues' presentations to attend, thus giving them some choice as well. The symposium offered an amazing chance to learn from one another, celebrate our year, and look toward the future with new insights and ideas. Teachers presented topics like project-based learning, developing a math academy, increasing academic discourse, improving staff and student wellness, and integrating technology into instruction.

In the end, 92 percent of the entire staff rated the approach to PD as effective or highly effective (the remaining 8 percent were neutral). Teachers across the board reflected on the benefits of the ability not only to choose paths but also to learn from colleagues about their passions.

Echoing what this chapter is about, one teacher wrote, "More than anything these days, educators need inspiration and a drive to keep going. We want to do more than survive; we want to thrive. Doing passion projects like this—and giving us time to do them—are what keep us going and thriving every day!"

Strategy #3: True PLCs

Another area to explore is if and how you do professional learning communities (PLCs) at your school. The use of PLCs could be either a great space to build in autonomy . . . or more micromanagement in disguise.

As PLCs evolved from concept to practice to buzzword, they quickly became the term du jour for any group of educators who meet regularly. I've heard the term for *PLC* used to describe

- Regular staff/department meetings.
- Meetings where staff are asked to review specific data.
- Meetings where teachers plan content for the next week.
- Times when administrators don't have anything else planned, so they say, "Meet in your PLCs" (which are just their departments or grade-level teams).

Even a cursory review of PLCs will bring you to DuFour's six Essential Characteristics (DuFour et al., 2016):

1. Shared mission, vision, values, and goals
2. Collaborative teams focused on learning
3. Collective inquiry
4. Action orientation and experimentation
5. Commitment to continuous improvement
6. Results oriented

Here lies the problem, though: Without doing deeper reading into these characteristics—and what they look like in practice—schools could consider just about any meeting a PLC. If the missions, goals, and values aren't *driven* by the educators themselves, PLCs lack both authenticity and autonomy. Put differently, telling a team of teachers to "analyze why your students are doing poorly on [standardized test standard]" is micromanagement, not a PLC.

PLCs have huge potential to support autonomy; however, one of the biggest mistakes I've seen districts make is rushing to do PLCs without the intentionality, time, and support needed to empower teachers. One district I worked with was antsy to go full tilt into PLCs the next year. Before the rollout, though, I used an efficacy ladder, which we will explore in Chapter 9, to help them break down the implementation into a timeline with subgoals. They quickly realized that, before they dove into full PLCs, there were steps like horizontal and vertical aligning that had to be done first (e.g., *what* was being taught).

Rather than rushing into PLCs, these school leaders made the intentional, teacher-supporting decision to slow down and focus on doing a few foundation-building steps first. The decision to focus on curriculum revisions not only prevented the district from adding a new (likely messy) initiative, but it also aligned with work teachers had already been requesting more time for. Thus, teachers were spared an increased workload *and* empowered with time to do work they already wanted to do.

Whole books have been written on how to create true PLCs, so if you're considering implementing (or revamping) your PLCs, I'd direct you to *Learning by Doing: A Handbook for Professional Learning Communities at Work* by DuFour et al. (2016) and *Facilitating Teacher Teams and Authentic PLCs: The Human Side of Leading People, Protocols, and Practices* by Daniel Venables (2017).

Strategy #4: Self-Concordant Goals

Schools often spend a lot of time developing their collective mission. Some school leaders also find value in establishing a tone or theme for a year. And there's a reason why: Collective focus on a mission or goal motivates our behavior, directs our actions, and serves as a destination worth pursuing.

So, what would it look like, then, if school leaders also made frequent time to meet with teachers about their *individual* goals for the year? Oftentimes, this is done early on in a teacher's career as a part of their individual development plan (IDP). However, this practice often drops off as teachers advance in their career. But goal striving shouldn't be a phase of a teacher's career or a hoop to jump through to get tenure. Helping a teacher set personally relevant goals is a powerful opportunity to build autonomy.

Setting self-concordant goals—personally meaningful goals—creates a host of benefits: increased well-being, greater likelihood of accomplishment, more long-term commitment, and boosted self-regard (Klug & Maier, 2014; Sheldon & Elliot, 1999). On the other hand, focusing on extrinsic goals (such as someone *telling* you what your goal is), is associated with higher anxiety, depression, narcissism, and physical illness (Kasser & Ryan, 1996). Oof. We should probably help people develop their own goals, then.

This strategy is simple yet powerful. At the beginning of the year, ask each staff member two questions:

- What's a professional goal or focus you want to work on this year?
- How can I support you with that goal?

And here are two important parts: First, follow up with the staff member about these questions. Informally discuss them when you check in with staff. Formally block out time in your schedule to meet one on one. Look for ways to connect staff members together around similar goals.

The second important part is to detach these goals from any form of evaluation. As soon as goals get tied to evaluation, they become extrinsic rather than intrinsic, and your efforts to discuss their goals will look more like surveillance than support. If autonomy is aligning one's actions to their choices, values, and interests, then let's help (a) figure out what those values and interests are and (b) make the choices to get that alignment.

Many schools that do individual development plans, unfortunately, make them "leader-fed" rather than "teacher-led" goals. Some of the most effective leaders I know use IDPs to leverage teacher choice and goal setting. These leaders might, for instance, suggest one goal but allow the teacher to select two that are personally relevant to them. They engage in dialogue to learn more about these goals (rather than treating IDPs as a checkbox to crank out), and in the process, they look for ways to link staff members who have similar goals, values, and interests.

* * *

Human motivation is a continuum of wild and wonderful. On the wild side, people are sometimes driven to abscond with a stranger's meatballs or chug a jar of formaldehyde. On the wonderful side, humans apply their signature strengths, innovate solutions, and rise above the adversities of life. The key to making it to the wonderful side is autonomy—not too much and not too little—but the chance to align one's actions to their goals and values. When the pressures rise, our instinct is to restrict and control and direct. But people need freedom. They need opportunity. They need trust. And trust—or the lack thereof—is the topic of our next burnout dimension and strengths-based solution.

PART III

Disconnected to Engaged

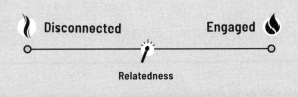

Disconnected   Engaged

Relatedness

6

Cynicism 101

We all have turning points in our lives. There's the day we get our driver's license—splitting our lives into before "vehicular freedom" and after. Before married life and after. Before babies (fur or human) and after.

The most recent turning point in my life has been "before I was prone to injury for no reason" and, now sadly, after. I've reached the age where falling asleep on the couch yields a three-day pinched nerve in my neck. A sneeze strains a back muscle. Standing up prompts joint pops and pain.

While these often feel like isolated events, each moment is a marker of our whole wellness—a symbolic symptom of our overall health: flexibility, inflammation, strength, cardiovascular efficiency, and more. These moments are not only a cue of the present; they are a culmination of all our previous health choices. Perhaps, then, the real change is not a shift from "healthy" to "unhealthy" but from "naiveté" to "wisdom."

When we're young, we ignore our body's cues, relying on a false optimism in our youthful ability to bounce back. But at a certain point we can't—or shouldn't—ignore these signs, no matter how small. We wise up to the cues our bodies have been giving us for decades: Drink more water and less booze. Get more sleep and have less screen time. Move more and eat less. Whether it's a strained joint, a spot on our skin, or a cough that won't quit, we live healthier, more resilient lives when we learn to listen and reflect on these signs. A wise person listens to the cues of their body. A wise leader listens to the cues of their organization.

So, what can a single moment tell us about the health of an organization?

I pondered this question after a friend of mine described an interaction with her administrators. During the peak of COVID, when the future of education was in flux, Mia (as we'll call her) was called down to her administrators' office and told to bring a union rep.

A tense conversation ensued, administration not pleased with Mia's cynicism and communication during staff interactions and Mia not pleased with administration's decisions and communication either. Through the attempted efforts of each party to feel heard, one line gouged Mia's memory when one of the administrator's said, "You just need to cut it out with all this negativity."

As Mia told me, "That was the moment when I was done. When they said *that,* it told me everything I needed to know about the school's culture."

I want to stop this thought train before it gets too close to Drama Town, because of course this single sentence is devoid of deeper context. Even I don't know the exact events leading up to the tense meeting. But a single transgression of cynicism is fodder *for* and information *on* the intensity of burnout. A cynical moment is the biopsy of an afflicted organ. It identifies the degree of infection and points to its future growth.

You might look at the sentence "cut it out with all this negativity" and picture moments when you wished a staff member *really would just knock off the negativity.* Maybe you *have* told someone to "knock it off" (or worse). We're not going to analyze the merits or malevolence of this sentence. Instead, we're going to look at what it represents:

- How does an individual get to a point where cynicism drives their outward behavior?
- How does a school leader see beyond the cynical transgressions, identifying the causes and conditions prompting it?

- How does a school leader reduce cynicism and increase engagement?

To eradicate the disease of cynicism, we will first look at the symptoms, followed by the causes. Then, in Chapter 7, we will explore how to treat and eradicate this organizational disease.

Cynicism Defined

We all have grouchy moments. But what differentiates between a rough day and genuine cynicism? Cynicism is defined as (1) a negative attitude that employees have toward their organization, (2) a belief that the organization lacks integrity, and (3) behavioral tendencies that are disparaging and critical of the organization (Atalay et al., 2022).

One challenge of identifying true cynicism is the cultural expectation called *toxic positivity*, the overgeneralization that we should be happy and optimistic across contexts. In our push for positive, resilient cultures, we sometimes mistake every moment of unpleasant emotion as cynicism. But education is a difficult profession and we care about doing well. So, we will naturally have moments of frustration when our efforts don't succeed. These moments of frustration—even if they are communicated publicly or unpleasantly—aren't necessarily cynicism.

Therefore, we shouldn't mistake every "puff of hot air" as a crisis. Just as not every headache is a brain tumor (despite how many times our hypochondriac readers have looked up brain tumor symptoms on WebMD).

But, like an effective doctor, we shouldn't ignore the puffs of hot air—we should explore further, adopting a Curiosity Mindset and looking for patterns. There are three components of organizational cynicism that serve as further symptoms:

1. **Cognitive Cynicism:** a belief that an organization lacks honesty and exploits its employees (Pfrombeck et al., 2020). For example, a sign of cognitive cynicism might be a staff member saying something like "We say we value the 'whole child' but only ever focus on test scores."

2. **Affective Cynicism:** reacting to the organization emotionally, feeling a combination of emotions like nervousness, anger,
   disgust, fear, or shame. If someone mentions feeling anxious or
   frustrated at the *idea* of coming to work, it's a sign of affective
   cynicism.
3. **Behavioral Cynicism:** criticizing the organization with sar-
   casm, verbally or nonverbally, and pessimistic predictions. An
   example here would be deflecting a new initiative with comments like "You wait, I bet in two years we'll move on to a new
   buzzword to obsess over."

Genuine cynicism, then, is more than a rough day. It's a pervasive, chronic feeling of negativity aimed at the organization, working
conditions, and individuals with whom we work. Investigating and
understanding cynicism is critical to the health and success of schools
because it is devastating to both individuals and cultures.

The Effects of Cynicism

On the individual level, cynicism leads to "diminished organizational
identification, lower levels of affective commitment, waning job satisfaction, and, ultimately, increased turnover" (Bedeian, 2007, 25).
Cynicism is like the other dimensions of exhaustion and inefficacy in
that it erodes a person's capacity and commitment to their career. But,
there are a number of key differences between cynicism and other
burnout dimensions.

Cynicism Is More Likely to Be Public

Whereas an individual's exhaustion or inefficacy is typically felt
internally and therefore silent to the organization, cynicism is often
expressed outwardly, thus potentially affecting (or infecting) others
in the school or community. If, for example, I am drained (exhaustion) or lack confidence (inefficacy), I'm probably just going to sit
silent during a staff meeting. If, however, I feel cynical, my behaviors
and emotions are more likely to express outwardly: complaints, sarcastic side comments, pointed questions, eye rolls, and more. On one

hand, we often get transparent evidence of cynicism. On the other hand, if we don't address the underlying symptoms, the public nature of cynicism increases its spread.

Cynicism Is Infectious

Because cynicism is often expressed publicly, it can erode the whole school culture. I can't, for example, make someone else more exhausted because I'm exhausted. I can't easily lower someone's efficacy with a strategy just because I lack efficacy. But I can make others feel cynical when I'm cynical.

Social scientists have demonstrated that our outward behavior and moods are socially contagious—not only affecting our immediate network but rippling out up to three degrees of influence (Christakis & Fowler, 2009). Cynicism has been proven to spread among teachers (Meredith et al., 2019). A cynical, sarcastic comment toward a colleague may sour their mood, thus affecting their students, who in turn may go home bitter around their family. It's no surprise then that, as organizational cynicism increases in teachers, school culture is negatively affected and student achievement diminishes—in part because of the erosion of culture and in part due to teachers lowering their expectations and performance in class (Karadağ et al., 2014). It is paramount that we stop the unpleasant transmission of cynicism. However, because it is an unpleasant transmission, many leaders don't combat it.

Cynicism Creates Emotional Distancing

Added to the contagion of cynicism is the challenge of its abrasive nature. If we imagine exhaustion as implosion, cynicism is combustion. Cynical responses, rooted in anger, fear, or distrust, often attack people or institutions. As such, if someone attacks us cynically, our default is defense: fight, flight, or freeze. If a teacher launches a snarky comment at me in a staff meeting, it's not easy for me to listen and explore with level-headedness and empathy. It's much easier to write them off as a jerk. Our desire to emotionally distance is the *opposite* response we should take to address cynicism: We must go against our survival instincts and rush into the flames, battling combustion with compassion.

You can see the compounding problem. Organizational cynicism not only ripples out to our culture but is difficult and unpleasant to address. I have to support someone who may have lashed out at me or the organization I represent. The very mindsets that are hardest to adopt when addressing cynicism are the ones we most need: Curiosity and Compassion.

I understand the struggle of understanding cynicism firsthand—of needing to adopt the very mindsets most damaged by cynicism. I've learned a key lesson that every school leader needs to remember: cynicism is fear masked in fury. One infamous staff meeting taught me this perspective the hard way.

The Golden Boy Gets Belted: A Key Lesson of Cynicism

During my second year teaching, I got a call from my superintendent. As her name flashed on my classroom phone, my armpits engaged pre-perspire mode. *Am I in trouble?* With a shaky voice, I picked up the phone, preparing for the pink slip. Then she surprised me: The newspaper wanted to interview me about dynamic teaching. They wanted to put me on the front page. They wanted to record an interview for their website to feature great young teachers. I wasn't in trouble. I was in the spotlight.

Despite still feeling like I had no idea what I was doing as a teacher, the interview went smoothly. The video of my teaching somehow made me look competent. I got calls and messages from friends and family all over the region, excited to see my face on the front cover of the Sunday paper. I remember feeling a sense of pride and relief that I had never felt in my life. And then we had a staff meeting.

My pride was quickly gouged as veteran colleagues spoke out in anger at our superintendent. I can still feel my shocked expression as I remember the comments that day—not only directed at our superintendent, but cynicism sprayed at me personally.

I know you want us all to teach like Chase, but I'm not going to jump around on tables in costume and play silly games all day like him.

Good for Chase and all, but I can't believe you featured a second-year instead of the rest of us.

It didn't stop after the meeting. A colleague approached me in the hallway. "It's great that you're doing all this stuff . . . but don't get used to it. I used to try that stuff too, but you'll lose your idealism soon. Enjoy it while it lasts." It was then that I learned staff referred to me pejoratively as "golden boy." I felt the personal, direct stabs of cynicism.

I'm not presenting this to you as a sob story of "poor ol' golden boy." I'm sharing this to frame a major bias I had toward the concept of cynicism. After receiving the blunt end of cynicism in my back, I held judgment to any moment I saw it—toward any person who showed it. My thinking was simple: "Cynics are crotchety curmudgeons who can't handle change." Perhaps you hold this bias too, having no doubt been the subject of cynicism in your time as an educator or school leader. Cynicism is easy to deflect as a salty response from even saltier people. We often hold a bias that is, ironically, cynical of cynicism.

Fast forward *many* years and a whole lot of research on cynicism (and forgiveness), and I realized one of the most important things we *all* need to know about cynicism.

Cynicism is a defense mechanism. It's a strategy employed to preserve energy, to protect oneself from disappointment, to create emotional distance. Cynicism is the "fight or flight" response of burnout. If, for example, I mock a new initiative as another buzzword fad of education, I apply defensive pessimism. I limit the energy I pour into something that actually might be gone in a couple years. I prevent myself from caring about something that might crush my spirit if it's ripped out from under me.

Let me be clear: The fact that cynicism is a defense mechanism is *not* an excuse for unprofessional behavior. We shouldn't take personal attacks on the chin or settle for apathy among our staff. Believe me— I still have my scars from cynicism directed at me personally. We aren't *accepting* cynicism. We are *analyzing* cynicism to better understand its roots. At the heart of cynicism is pain. It's broken trust. It's the smoldering ashes of extinguished hope.

At its core, cynicism is a wicked combination of exhaustion and damaged relationships. A cynical person doesn't want to expend energy to change—sometimes attacking those who imply they *should* change—because past experience and damaged relationships have eroded trust, empathy, and connectedness. This is key to adopting the Curiosity and Compassion Mindsets necessary to address cynicism. When I have the compassionate understanding that cynicism stems from mistrust and preserving energy—and when I explore the source of these feelings with curiosity—I address the issue at the source, not just the symptom.

Next, we will explore the primary causes of cynicism so we can rebuild relationships and reduce or halt the spread of cynical mindsets in our individuals and our cultures.

Nature or Nurture: A Distracting Debate

A quick aside on a thought that lingers anytime I talk to school leaders or staff on the topic of cynicism. Are some people just Debbie Downers—destined to declare doom on anything new? And, if so, should we avoid hiring them or, at the least, stuff them in a corner of the building to live like a troll? Let's explore.

Are certain personality types and temperaments heritable? To some extent, yes. We have genetic predispositions to things like having a pessimistic versus an optimistic explanatory style. Twin studies have shown that genetics account for 40–60 percent of the heritability of the "Big Five" personality types (openness, conscientiousness, extroversion, agreeableness, neuroticism) (Power & Pluess, 2015). In short, yes, some people are born having to work harder at optimism or flexibility to change. But these predispositions are neither destiny nor doom. The "nurture" side of life has a huge influence on how these traits develop over time. And the field of epigenetics is showing that our contexts and choices can influence the degree to which heritable traits take hold of our life.

But let's get cynical and imagine what it would look like if we assumed cynicism was a set-in-stone personality type—and therefore we wanted to select teachers who weren't genetically grouches. First, good luck trying to make "personality surveys" a valid, reliable (and ethical) part of your hiring and evaluation process. However, even if you use a reliable, validated measure, like the Big Five personality survey, this "fixed personality" is fraught with issues.

For example, it's true that cynicism and burnout *are* linked to scoring high on "neuroticism" scales (Syed & Syed, 2013). Therefore, one could argue that, if we want to reduce burnout and increase retention, we should avoid hiring people who are anxious, depressed, or prone to emotional volatility, right? Here's the kicker: If we're selecting personalities to reduce burnout, then we also must avoid choosing folks high in conscientiousness—because people who plan, organize, prioritize, and give attention to details are also more likely to burn out, especially when the organization lacks role clarity (Venkatesh et al., 2021). At best, it's nebulous to make personality types a major factor in our hiring and retention decisions.

Focusing on cynicism as a product of personality is detrimental to our efforts to empower educators; it puts the onus and blame on the character of the individual rather than the contexts and culture of our schools. Like burnout more generally, we don't reduce cynicism until we recognize that it is a *response* to working conditions. We don't blame the afflicted organ for the disease. We eradicate the conditions that give rise to the disease.

How Cynicism Develops

We know that cynicism has key symptoms. We know that it is a psychological defense that becomes a cultural disease, eroding personal engagement and productive teams. So where does it stem from? While many different conditions can cause cynicism, most of them fall under one of these three "viruses" of burnout.

The Viruses of Cynicism: Perceived Unfairness, Value Mismatches, and Loss of Community

Virus: Perceived Unfairness

Imagine you tell a new hire that you'll pay them a certain salary. Then, upon working, you pay them less. You could imagine that breaking this contract would give any employee the right to feel angry and distrusting toward your organization. We'd deem this experience unfair. No one would fault the employee if they gave subpar work, since what they were promised was not upheld fairly. If we can understand the effects of a broken written contract, then we can understand the effects of a broken psychological contract—and how both can lead to cynicism.

Organizational research has demonstrated that a major source of cynicism in the workplace is broken psychological contracts (Li & Chen, 2018). Psychological contracts are the expectations, beliefs, and obligations between an employee and their employer. When they are broken, individuals lose trust with the organization because they perceive it to be dishonest and unfair, damaging the quality of the relationship and, in turn, leading to cynicism.

Psychological contracts are sometimes explicit, although they can also be implicit. Here are some examples of seemingly minor but psychologically major breaches in trust:

Explicitly Broken:

- Telling a teacher they will only have two preps next year but then giving them more when the school year starts.
- Promising that you'll dedicate time and resources to an initiative but not following through.

Implicitly Broken:

- Creating vision statements that express the value of teaching to the whole child but then spending all professional development time focusing on test score data.
- Requiring your staff to respond to emails within 24 hours but not responding to their emails within the same time frame.

No doubt, there are moments when expectations get broken by things beyond a school leader's control—perhaps they promise a teacher two preps, but then another teacher quits mid-year, leaving gaps that need to be filled. Maybe a leader *wants* to focus on whole-child support, but the school board puts massive pressure on leadership to analyze academics due to a recent dip in test scores.

If factors beyond our control disrupt our intentions, then we have essentially two options: (1) stop making promises we can't guarantee and (2) work extra hard to build relational capital with our staff to bolster against unexpected breaches. The latter will be the subject of Chapter 7. Analogously, we can't control the weather. But we at least shouldn't promise it won't storm, and we should make sure our houses are built on sturdy foundations to weather the storm if it comes.

Trust isn't just a person-to-person experience; it hovers within our culture as well. Employees compare their work experience to their peers, gauging if the organization treats them (or others) fairly. Maslach's research has shown perceived unfairness to be one of the major causes of burnout—and it's a cause that seems to be growing in organizations (Moss, 2021).

Let's admit that, in complex organizations, there is no such thing as 100 percent fair—people will get paid different amounts for different levels and types of work, even with collective bargaining agreements and common pay scales. Evaluations will differ, even if teachers have similar students and curriculum. But we should still seek equitable practices and consistency with our policies to greatly reduce unfairness. And we should analyze if our practices are favoring individuals at the expense of others in the community.

One example is "teacher of the year" practices. In the education sphere, public praise has undertones of control—we often praise individuals as a behavior control for groups ("I *love* how Susie is sitting quietly at her table. Thank you, Susie"). The hidden message people perceive is "If you want to be acknowledged like Teacher X, you need to teach like Teacher X." Are our praise practices genuinely for acknowledging excellence, or are they a "carrot" of motivation—a control in disguise? And, if they *are* for genuine acknowledgment, are there better ways to give people praise?

Additionally, sometimes these good intentions aren't even wanted. For example, for a while, our administration tried bestowing a teacher of the year parking space. Beyond the issue of individual awards creating tension (whispers of "golden boy" haunt the author as he writes), it was a flawed practice because most of the teachers—including winners—parked in a completely different lot. They got the awkwardness of jealous stares without the meaningful prize. The psychological losses of the public award far outweighed the benefits.

Juxtapose this idea to a different idea our district tried. Rather than giving a teacher of the year award, they acknowledged the entire school staff by hosting an end-of-year carnival. An overwhelmingly well-received event, the carnival was a chance for the entire staff to feel acknowledged and supported while building social connectedness across the whole staff.

In the interest of not promoting an "everyone gets a trophy" agenda, I want to stress that we shouldn't *avoid* acknowledging individuals for their unique talents and contributions. Instead, we should *adjust* the delivery of this acknowledgment. Praise groups in public; praise individuals in private. In the next chapter, we'll explore more ideas for acknowledging individuals in ways that improve the culture rather than damage trust and fairness.

Our actions speak loudly about the trustworthiness and fairness of our organization. If we say we're going to do something, we better (a) make sure we follow through and (b) make sure our actions do more psychological good than harm.

Virus: Values Mismatch

Christina Maslach and her colleagues refer to the causes of burnout as *mismatches*: My workload doesn't match the time and resources I have. My leader's words don't match their actions. Among these mismatches is one that has a huge influence on cynicism—a mismatch between my values and the work I do.

Our values are one of—if not *the*—biggest intrinsic motivators for this profession. When our values don't match the work or they actively go against the work we're being asked to do, it erodes our motivation. And it disenchants us from our profession as we think, "This job doesn't allow me to do what I think is best."

Additionally, education is knowledge work, making it more susceptible to value mismatches. When I worked in a factory that made street signs between semesters of college, I didn't have many value conflicts. I churned out street signs. They paid me. I went home. I didn't have conflict with colleagues on differing philosophies of how to make street signs. I didn't have community members attacking me on social media for indoctrinating street signs with my political views.

Contrast that to the complex, value-driven work of education. Consider all the different values that a teacher has within their work; then, consider to what extent those values may mismatch the values or actions of other stakeholders: students, parents, colleagues, community members, and school leadership. Here is an abridged list of areas where value mismatches could emerge:

- Teacher values the learning process; student values the grade.
- Teacher values ownership; student values not getting in trouble.
- Teacher values depth of knowledge; curriculum requires breadth.
- Teacher values social-emotional needs of students; school values test scores.
- Teacher values communication; parent doesn't respond to calls or emails.
- Teacher values curriculum A; colleagues value curriculum B.
- Teacher values respect of the profession; social media posts suggest teachers are the problem.
- Teacher values adding arts electives; administration values adding science electives.
- Teacher values autonomy; policies promote micromanagement and control.
- Teacher values regular feedback; evaluation process only provides feedback at the end of the year.
- Teacher values open communication; administration doesn't implement systems for keeping staff informed.

And we could go on. I don't show this list to overwhelm you; instead, I offer this sample to emphasize the importance of our Illuminating Mindsets. A Curiosity Mindset requires us to learn more about our staff's values and needs. A Compassion Mindset pushes us to understand where our colleagues are coming from—and how our values might be more aligned than we thought. A Creativity Mindset encourages us to seek effective solutions for increasing autonomy or revising policies and practices so that diverse needs are met.

We can also address the issue of value mismatches with a Compass Mindset: What are the productive values that I want my teachers to adopt in this school? How do our organizational practices support those values—through hiring, retention efforts, communication, professional development, and more? And, if we truly *say* we value something, do our actions show it consistently? As Ralph Waldo Emerson wrote in *Letters and Social Aims*, "Don't say things. What you are stands over you the while, and thunders so that I cannot hear what you say to the contrary."

Burnout vs. Demoralization

A surge of conversation has emerged about the difference between burnout and demoralization. As we've mentioned, burnout is a chronic condition of workplace stress, characterized by exhaustion, cynicism, and inefficacy.

Demoralization, as expert Doris Santoro (2018) explains, is "dissatisfaction that occurs when teachers encounter consistent and pervasive challenges to enacting the values that motivate their work." Teachers who feel demoralized feel like the mandates they must follow are "harmful to students or degrading to the profession and that their attempts to alter them have been fruitless" (para. 3).

So, what's the difference? Demoralization stems from similar value mismatches that can also lead to burnout. Reviewing the list above of sample value mismatches, one could see how the intensity of a value mismatch could make a teacher feel demoralized. For example, I can recall two colleagues who quit the profession primarily because of value mismatches—both had exceptional efficacy, positive communities, and no problem managing workloads. They simply reached a point where their values (e.g., addressing equity issues; adopting progressive evaluation practices), and the educational system were too mismatched.

Did they quit because of burnout or demoralization? One could argue that they quit because of demoralization, but had they stayed they possibly would have become cynical and burned out. But I don't think we have time to get hung up on semantics. Whether you are looking at it through the lens of burnout or demoralization, two things are key:

1. We must focus on addressing systemic working conditions that create value mismatches.
2. Unresolved value mismatches damage good teachers, whether the result is lingering with cynicism or leaving due to demoralization.

Virus: Loss of Community

Reflecting on burnout thus far, one major concept should stand out: burnout stems from imbalances. For example, with emotional exhaustion, I have too much workload and not enough autonomy, time, or skill to lift me over the challenge. With cynicism, I have an imbalance of negative versus positive experiences with my organization. For example, I may have had a lot of moments of distrust and damaged expectations and not enough moments of positive and secure relationships to lift me to renewed hope and resilience. Our next virus, loss of community, might not *cause* cynicism, but it allows cynicism to fester unchallenged.

Education, a highly social profession, is a field susceptible to the impact of weakened social connection. The success of our day hinges upon the social interactions within our school, so it's no surprise that lack of community or social connectedness has strong correlations with burnout; the less a person feels connected to their students, their colleagues, and their leadership, the more likely they are to feel burnout (O'Brennen et al., 2017). Even seemingly minor social damage can impact our work—one study found that a single "micro-exclusion" can lead to an immediate 25 percent drop in an individual's performance with a team (Deloitte Insights, 2020). And, as mentioned in Chapter 1, teachers of color are far more likely to cite feeling unwelcome in school communities as they often deal with prejudice and micro-exclusions compared to their white peers (Dixon et al., 2019).

Consider, then, the impact of COVID-19 on our school communities. In every district I worked with the past few years, school leaders spoke of the emotional distance at their schools during the pandemic.

On a direct level, school closures, virtual learning, and hybrid learning created physical distance. We couldn't even see the people we work with in person. Even in person, masks impaired socialization, and we couldn't accurately read facial expressions—couldn't see full smiles. And then there was the emotional loss of community as political differences wedged into the fabric of our day, whether it was staff disagreements or community anger about school safety policies and curricula. The distance was felt physically and emotionally.

Without social connection, our schools suffer. For example, relational trust, the glue of social connection, is strongly connected to school performance. One study found that in top-quartile schools,

> three-quarters of teachers reported strong or very strong relations with fellow teachers, and nearly all reported such relations with their principals. By contrast, at schools in the bottom quartile, a majority of teachers having little or no trust in their colleagues, two-thirds said the same about their principals, and fewer than 40 percent reported positive, trusting relations with parents. (EL Education, 2015, para. 8)

Schools with strong levels of trust had a 1-in-2 chance of making significant improvements in math and reading. Schools with weak trust only had a 1-in-7 chance of making gains. Strong trust and strong community connections go hand in hand.

Conversely, when we *have* strong social connectedness, it's a boon for both our staff and our students. Having social support during a challenging situation increases activation of the parasympathetic nervous system, activates the reward center, and releases oxytocin, which increases social cognition, affiliation, interpretation of facial expressions, and feelings of trustworthiness (Southwick & Southwick, 2020). For students, the more positive the relational balance between teacher and student, the higher student engagement is (Martin & Collie, 2018).

Social connection, then, is the immune system of our schools. When it is present, we have defenses against adversity. We have positive interactions to make up for the negative. We have trust to do what's best for kids. We have colleagues and a community to pick us up when we're down. But when social connection is down, our system is ripe for the rot and disease of cynicism.

Now that we know how to identify the disease of cynicism, we need to focus on solutions. Saying, "Cut it out!" is no more effective in eradicating cynicism as it is in eradicating pneumonia. And yet, when it comes to dealing with cynicism, our strategies aren't much more diversified or sophisticated than telling someone to stop being negative. We blame the patient rather than treating the disease.

We have to see cynicism for what it really is: a deterioration of intrinsic motivation due to broken trust, mismatched values, and a loss of community. Cynicism is a defense mechanism of an organism saving energy because it has been damaged too many times. It's a symptom of systemic issues—one that, if we approach it with curiosity and compassion, we can stop from spreading and save the individual.

We can't stop every condition giving rise to cynicism. Much of the negativity a teacher experiences may be beyond a school leader's control. But we can create an immune system of support that reduces its odds and increases our ability to fight negativity with resilience, hope, and community. In our next chapter, we boost the immune system of relatedness.

7

Relatedness

Parent-teacher conferences almost killed me. Not as in "that was tiring, so I'm whiny" kind of killed me. As in "hospitalized and moments away from a feeding tube" kind of killed me.

In 2014, I came home from our spring parent-teacher conferences. It was 8:30 p.m., and I grabbed my celebratory beer for surviving another night of the "extraversion extravaganza" that exhausts us introverts. As I took my first sip, a dull pain started in my chest. I assumed it was heartburn because, y'know, "aging."

The next day it intensified. Everything I ate—everything I drank, even water—sent sharp, searing pain down my esophagus. Going on day two, I was without food or water, admitted to the hospital, and hooked up to an IV. To numb my esophagus and allow me to eat ice chips, I chugged a pale pink drink labeled "magic mouthwash" (which, to my disappointment, gave me no powers of levitation or telepathy). Doctors scoped my throat, which they described as looking like "ground beef" (gross as that analogy is, my stomach growled for a cheeseburger). I was six days without food, hours away from a feeding tube, when my system started to heal for reasons unknown. Two days later, I was released from the hospital and headed straight to a burger shop.

OK, maybe I'm a little dramatic about the "almost dying" thing. I'm thankful that I had great hospital care throughout this time. To this day, though, I (and the medical staff) don't know what happened to my throat. Their best guess is that I caught a virus from someone, which I have no choice but to assume was from a parent during conferences (conveniently supporting my "p-t conferences are the worst" introversion bias).

The real marvel of this experience is the power of the human immune system. A team of doctors, nurses, and medical staff couldn't identify the threat. But my body did. As we move about the world, working and worrying and wondering, our immune system battles on our behalf. Each day, our bodies fight viruses and smite bacteria that seep into our system. Each day, it engineers antibodies to defeat future foes.

We will never eradicate all the viruses, toxins, fungi, and bacteria that surround us. So we must boost our immune system, fueling it with the vitamins, rest, and resources it needs.

And we will never eradicate all the challenges and conditions that create cynicism. Therefore, we must build up our school's "social immune system" so that, when negativity and pessimism attempt to spread like a virus, the power of our culture eradicates its growth. In this chapter, we explore the key strategies to build a strong, cohesive culture—strategies that not only *reduce* cynicism but also *boost* the positive connection of our people.

The Power of Vitamin R: Relatedness

Human beings are not the biggest creatures. We aren't the fastest, the most agile, or, as Facebook feeds have shown, always the brightest animals in the kingdom. Our success as a species didn't spring from what is *within* us. We succeed because of what is *between* us. It is our relatedness—our ability to collaborate, to support, to work together—that allows us to thrive. And science supports this.

To understand the power of human connection, we can first look at its opposite: isolation. Despite the rise of technology and networks of social media, isolation is a felt experience. We can be surrounded by people and still feel alone. And this lack of social connection can be devastating. While obesity reduces longevity by 20 percent, drinking by 30 percent, and smoking by 50 percent, loneliness reduces our longevity by 70 percent (Seppala & King, 2021). Isolation is also linked with exhaustion: The more exhausted a person is, the more isolated they feel.

Conversely, feeling socially connected strengthens our immune system, boosts our lifespan, and reduces anxiety and depression. On the school front, students who feel relatedness at school have greater academic performance, better attendance, greater mental health, and stay in school longer (CDC, n.d.). For staff, social connection creates a buffer for burnout in school leaders (Beausaert et al., 2016). It reduces teacher burnout, serving as a critical work resource (Szabo & Jagodics, 2019).

All this suggests that, if we want to reduce cynicism, we should adopt a Compass Mindset. Beyond reducing negative working conditions, we should look to build positive conditions by actively increasing social connection. Connected cultures *can* happen without our intervention, just as our immune system can work innately. However, the more we fuel our systems with what they need, the greater our organizational (and physical) health. Figure 7.1 shows the six "vitamins" we can give our cultures to reduce cynicism and build relatedness.

Staff Rapport

There are multiple dimensions of social capital that must be built. Each stakeholder should feel positive connections to every other stakeholder, whether it's staff to student, leadership to community, or something else. For the purposes of our focus—staff well-being—we'll emphasize the two most important:

- Staff to staff.
- Leader to staff.

Staff rapport is critical. Our social supports—namely our sense of community—form one of the greatest buffers from burnout (Asensio-Martínez et al., 2017).

It's important to note, though, that connectedness does not always imply *positive* connections that improve school communities. For

FIGURE 7.1

The Social Six

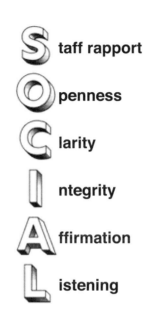

example, staff might be well connected, but if their cynicism levels are high, then burnout and discontent can spread faster—much the way our interconnected systems in our bodies can allow cancer to metastasize. When we talk about staff rapport here, then, we are talking about relationships between colleagues that allow for safety, support, and belonging. And although there are many ways to promote staff rapport, one of the most powerful moves you can make is creating and encouraging traditions.

Vitamin Supplement: Create Traditions

Traditions are a wellspring for positive relationships: (a) they involve groups of people meeting together; (b) they build bonds over common experiences; and (c) they amplify positive emotion on three chronemic levels—we look forward to them (future), we experience joy in the moment (present), and we reflect on them (past).

Traditions can be tricky to start and maintain (as my mom can tell you from attempting dozens of family traditions that never stuck). In a school setting, I've found the following elements are key:

1. There is more than one "keeper of the tradition"—preferably staff and not only school leaders.
2. They don't take a lot of time, use excess energy, or push workloads back onto a teacher's schedule (see Figure 7.2).
3. They are inclusive to everyone.
4. They involve joy, gratitude, or affirmation.
5. They involve food.

OK, that last one might not be required, but food is the glue that keeps most traditions together. Here are some of my favorite traditions that I've used, experienced, or heard.

Staff Shout-Outs: Periodically, invite staff to submit a "shout-out" to a colleague who has had a positive effect at school. I use a quick Google form and ask nominators to note a person, provide a reason, and select whether they want this person to be acknowledged publicly or privately. I collect the public shout-outs, put them on the same document or email, and then send it out for the whole staff. If it's private, I email the nominee with a note: "Someone wanted to acknowledge you because. . . ."

Pass the Praise: Kick the "administrator's pet" award and let staff acknowledge each other. Ask someone to nominate a peer or colleague who has done something positive. Then bestow the acknowledgment and award. Between then and the next meeting, a recipient must identify another peer they want to pass the praise to. In my previous district, we utilized a coffee mug as the "award," and nominators could stuff it with gifts or notes if they chose.

Cookouts and Potlucks: Here's where we bring the power of food. During many staff development days, once the lunch break hits, people scramble off campus in various groups to grab lunch. It's a great chance to bond; however, it's also a great chance to introduce a tradition.

FIGURE 7.2

It's a Trap! Why Team Building Rarely Works

We were on question number six when the nonverbal cues of discontent commenced—shuffling and subtle groaning. Sighs and sideways glances. A teacher near me uttered, "I could be grading essays instead of doing this."

The leadership team wanted to mix it up at a staff meeting and play a game where people made predictions on categories like "greatest movie." Whichever one had the most votes got a point (e.g., if *Titanic* was the most popular choice, anyone who wrote *Titanic* got the point). It was a lot of fun . . . for the first five rounds. After we realized that we were doing a dozen rounds—encompassing the whole of our staff meeting—the good intentions of team building turned into more of a time suck.

Team building is a phrase inflated to the point of little meaning. And it's a go-to strategy from school leaders that often misses the mark. Here's why team building largely fails:

1. **It lacks real focus.** Much of the time, team building is just a random game or activity. Sure, it can create moments of joy or play, but if that's it, then call it a game and treat it as such. If there *is* an intended purpose, make that overt. Are we building creative problem-solving skills? Increasing communication and listening skills? Developing empathy? And if we *are* developing a specific skill, then we have to consider the second flaw with most team building.
2. **It doesn't translate to teaching practice.** Much of the team building I've observed—with staff or with students—is 90 percent activity and 10 percent (at best) reflection and connection to real life. If we want a team-building experience to be meaningful, then we must plan for intentional debriefs to distill purposeful change. In Appendix B, I provide a framework called "The Whats" for pulling meaning out of virtually any experience, whether it's a team-building activity or reflecting on a challenge. To properly reflect and change, team building requires a valuable commodity that we don't often have to spare: time.
3. **It consumes valuable time.** I'll take this opportunity to mention from my megaphone, yet again, the "zero-sum rule": don't add new workloads until you reduce existing workloads. If we do a 30-minute team-building exercise at a staff meeting, it shouldn't require that I now have to spend 30 minutes of my own time responding to forms or planning work that we *could* have accomplished in the meeting. If we're doing a staff ropes course at the beginning of the year, I hope I've still been given adequate time to set up my classroom and review new policy changes.

For the reasons above, I'm skeptical any time I hear "team building" as an approach to building staff relatedness. Absolutely, team building can be done effectively and transform the community within a school. However, when time is scarce or the team-building focus is unclear, opt for strategies that create positive emotions like joy, reflection, and affirmation without taking up too much time.

At least a couple times a year, we used one of the development days for a potluck. In mid-winter, we usually hosted a chili cook off. Last fall we did a "Dip Competition." No matter the theme, potlucks and cookouts are a chance to bring people together over a meal and share things they love—whether it's their recipes or the family stories and traditions behind them.

Evenings for Educators: One of my favorite traditions I've been a part of lately is "Evening for Educator" events. Many districts and ISDs are organizing specific evenings to honor their educational staff. These events often collaborate with local businesses who offer discounts or promotional prizes—things like restaurants, shops, gym memberships, and cleaning services. I've spoken at many of these events, and they are among the most refreshing traditions: seeing educators come together to experience joy, affirmation, and reminders that we are not alone and that this work matters. While it takes a bit more legwork than a potluck, the connections are well worth the investment.

There's a key lesson of staff relatedness: Just because we get groups of people together, it doesn't mean that positive relatedness is happening. For true connection to happen, there must be a source of joy, affirmation, and common understanding. Traditions are your go-to move for this source of social capital.

Openness

Pause your reading for a moment and direct your attention to your heart. Maybe take your pulse. Take some deep breaths to feel your heart slow. Hold your hand to your chest. This 10-ounce lump of muscle makes life as you know it function.

Like many of your organs, the heart works best when there is no obstruction. Your heart cycles through blood, accepting and delivering. Accepting and delivering. Accepting and delivering. If either the acceptance or the delivery is blocked, then the functioning of your body stalls—or worse.

If a school's community is the body, then you, the school leader, are the heart—and open communication is the blood. Our second source of social capital is the trust and mutual growth that stems from *openness*. Here, like the heart, we are being open in two directions:

1. Accepting feedback.
2. Delivering clear communication.

The latter we will address in our next section. Here, we are going to narrow in on the role of welcoming feedback.

Vitamin Supplement: Request Feedback

The most effective leaders—and people—I know invite feedback beyond formalized and required methods. In other words, the district-provided, end-of-the-year survey isn't their primary source of information on how to improve their craft and community as leaders.

Illuminating leaders build feedback into the fabric of their culture so that it is timely, authentic, and actionable. Accepting and implementing feedback is also a key way to show respect for staff—giving them voice in decisions and directions that affect them, which leads to lower cynicism (Manne, 2012). Additionally, seeking support for reducing burnout has been proven to reduce cynicism and burnout in general, as teachers engage in proactive coregulation (Pietarinen et al., 2021). However, if you haven't made feedback a regular part of your world, here are tips to make it worthwhile. Because I clearly love a good acronym, let's focus on the FACTS of effective feedback.

1. Followed Through

The most important part of asking for feedback is finding ways to act on it. If we aren't willing to change based on feedback, then we shouldn't bother asking. Many educators are wary of "feedback facade"—when leaders say they value feedback but never use it. Doing so *increases* cynicism because we damage trust in our leadership and the organization.

Do you have to then change *everything* someone suggests? Absolutely not. But here, a little bit of openness can build a lot of social capital. Here's the best move: If you ask for feedback at a staff meeting, review the feedback afterwards, and then, at the next meeting, summarize some of your big insights—which key ideas will you implement right away and which might you have to adapt to meet them halfway (or explore more before making a decision). This openness of communication makes people feel heard, adds transparency, and models commitment to growth.

2. Anonymous

Educators have hesitancy at first when being asked for feedback—they worry that, if they give unflattering feedback, it will be held against them. Assuage this fear by starting with anonymous feedback. While it's beneficial to have impromptu systems, like a feedback box in the staff lounge, these efforts often fail because we often forget about them (especially if there isn't any regular follow-through).

Instead, consider having regular prompted moments for feedback. For example, have staff fill out a feedback form or reflection question at each staff meeting. Or schedule an email to go out once a month (or more frequently) with a feedback form.

Over time, once staff see a school leader regularly follows through with feedback (and doesn't go ballistic if feedback is unflattering), there will be no need for anonymity, which ultimately is the goal.

3. Compassionate

We know the value of a Compassionate Mindset already. Feedback is a great time to put it to practice. Remember that every communication event is information—even if it's unflattering, it's still information. The root of feedback is reconciling a conflict or problem. So, here's a key mentality for embracing feedback: If feedback upsets you—which you're entitled to feel—focus on the *problem,* not the person. For example, consider a biting bit of feedback like "I'm sick of you changing our schedule at the last minute all the time." Sure, our dear colleague could've used a little (or a lot) more tact. But identify the problem. Last-minute communication is causing anxiety and stress. In this case, we can't change people, but we can change our communication. Focusing on the former fuels frustration, and the latter leads to solutions.

4. Timely

In Chapter 2, I mentioned how useless it felt to give professors end-of-term feedback forms in college—there was no chance for a professor to *act* on the feedback for the students offering it. Just as timely feedback is critical for student learning, it's critical to build positive relationships.

But here's the rub: Don't act on feedback *immediately* after receiving it. One recurring event has taught me this: the sub report. Every time I would come back to class after being out, I would read the sub report first thing in the morning. If it was bad, unpleasant emotions tainted my thoughts, leading me to be grouchier and harsher with students than I should be.

Provide yourself space—at least 24 hours—between receiving feedback and communicating with others about how you might integrate it. Let your brain grapple with ideas, process solutions, and—most of all—regulate disruptive emotions. But, after your cooling period, be sure to promptly summarize to staff the feedback you've received and the action steps you'll take.

5. Specific

When I first made it a regular routine for students to give me feedback, I felt deflated by their responses. They would write things like "Teach better" or "Nothing"—what do you do with that? By persisting and tweaking my feedback process, I've learned a couple tricks that have given me more quality feedback, all of which involve prompting specifics. Here are my top two suggestions:

- **Use categories.** Identify what aspects you need better feedback on and build those as categories for feedback. For example, you could use our SOCIAL acronym as categories, prompting staff to give you feedback on how you can improve staff rapport, openness, clarity, integrity, affirmation, and listening.
- **Use Likert scales.** Within categories, ask your staff to rate you on a scale. Then prompt qualitative feedback by asking, "What is one specific thing I can do to bump up a level on this scale?"

For example, when I implemented these with students, I asked questions like

- On a scale of 1–5, how helpful is the feedback I'm giving you on your essays? (1 = not at all helpful; 5 = very helpful)
- What is one thing I can do to give better feedback?

Combining categories with Likert scales gave me more timely, specific, and actionable feedback, which is key to effective growth.

If we want our organizations to be healthy and our staff to feel connected and fueled, then we need to function like the heart: accepting communication and feedback just as much as delivering it.

Clarity

Lack of clarity can be a major source of stress. If I'm unclear of my work expectations, at best, I have no way to measure my own effectiveness (damaging my efficacy). At worst, I fall into work traps I never knew were there (increasing my stress).

Beyond being a source of inefficacy and stress, ambiguity is a breeding ground for cynicism. Ambiguity allows for inconsistency, which conceives broken trust, which yields cynicism. Poor communication is a cause of cynicism, particularly for those who most identify with our organization (Sguera et al., 2021). If we want to reduce cynicism and build strong connections, clarity is key—in our roles, our relationships, and our communication.

Taking extra time to reflect on our word choice is one way to be clear (maybe reread that email before you hit send). However, beyond the day-to-day clarity of interpersonal communication, we also have to look at organizational communication to ensure that roles are clearly defined.

For example, in my third year as an instructional coach, I saw an email from our union president. It was a list of what topics they had discussed with administration on behalf of union members. Buried within the list, between things like mask protocols and subbing on plan periods, was this: "Is Chase an administrator? Admin says, 'Yes and no.'"

Dear reader, I wish you could have seen how wide my eyes got at this line. I had never been told I was an administrator. I sure wasn't being paid as an administrator. I didn't even know this question was on anyone's mind. What followed was yours truly on a mission to solve the mystery of Mr. Mielke's role.

In the end, I had to meet with school principals, union reps, and my superintendent to clearly define my role and responsibilities as a district instructional coach—clarifying that I wouldn't, for example, be a part of evaluating my colleagues, something I advocated for strongly.

Role ambiguity is more than a moment that freaked out Chase Mielke. Ambiguity is a major source of burnout, particularly for teachers (Schwab & Iwanicki, 1982). We saw in Chapter 6 how role conflict—when our values don't align with the actions of our role—can cause cynicism. But we also must make sure we don't have role ambiguity. Do our staff members know exactly what is expected of them and each other? And how do we know that they know? Our next power move can help us strengthen clarity in multiple ways.

Vitamin Supplement: Clarity T-Chart

In general, to increase clarity we can take extra time to reflect on our word choice. However, we can also increase clarity of our communication and our roles using what I call a Clarity T-Chart.

An irony of clarity is that sometimes we aren't clear if we are unclear. We go about our communication, not knowing how it is being interpreted, lived, or carried out by those we lead.

A Clarity T-Chart helps us draw a clear line between what is clear and what is unclear: On one side, people reflect on what *is* clear. On the other, we note what *isn't*. For example, let's imagine you are introducing a new plan to have teachers mentor struggling students (hopefully you've eliminated another initiative first, yeah?). After explaining it to staff, you hand them a half-sheet in which they respond to the prompts in Figure 7.3.

This form of feedback helps clarity on two levels. You'll get feedback on what still needs clarity (e.g., people write, "I'm not sure how often we are supposed to meet with these students"). However, you can also see what may have been misinterpreted—where they *think*

FIGURE 7.3

Clarity T-Chart

What I understand this initiative will require me to do:	What I still need more clarity on:

there's clarity, but it's still murky (e.g., staff wrote they thought they were mentoring any student they wanted, whereas your student support team wants them to mentor academically struggling students). Having both bits of information allows you to reduce ambiguity that you wouldn't have caught otherwise.

Another variation of the Clarity T-Chart is reducing role ambiguity. We used this in my previous district to delineate the responsibilities of four roles: instructional coaches versus interventionists versus teacher mentors versus administrators. Creating a column for each role, we broke down who was responsible for what. Not only did this allow clarity for those in the roles, but it also then served as a document to communicate with staff: "Here is what each person does so you know how to get the support you need."

Cynicism lurks in the shadows of ambiguity. Clarity T-Charts can shine a light on confusion so we can move forward with trust and understanding.

Integrity

If ambiguity creates shadows for cynicism to lurk, lack of integrity is fuel that feeds the beast. When people see our organizations—or us personally—as lacking integrity, it's a simple (and justifiable) conclusion that they will become cynical. Why would I spend mental or emotional energy for a system or person I do not trust?

Ultimately, this is what we are talking about with integrity: do the members of my school trust my actions? "There are only two ways you can damage or breach trust: Say you'll do something but you don't. Say you won't do something but then you do" (Kieschnick & Kieschnick, 2020). In this quote, my good friends the Kieschnicks break down an abstract idea—trust—into its most simplified form: integrity is aligning our actions with our words and values.

Consider how we maintain (or break) integrity in explicit and implicit ways. Explicit integrity breaks are a stab to the back; implicit integrity breaks are poison—less visible but just as damaging. If I say we aren't going to adopt a new learning management software next year, and then come August we're two days deep into learning one, then we have an explicit breach of trust: I said one thing, but I did another. Break the integrity, break the trust. And with no trust, there is no base for social capital.

When people use terms like *social capital*, they often discuss deposits and withdrawals. Positive interactions deposit social capital, and challenges withdraw social capital. As long as your balance remains positive, social connection should be strong. But breaking integrity isn't simply a withdrawal—it's robbery. It's a cleared bank account. Therefore, we should know *clearly* how much social capital is in our bank account. We do this with integrity checks.

Vitamin Supplement: Integrity Checks

Many of the strategies throughout this book will naturally build trust, such as increasing autonomy, having clear communication, and being open to feedback (Blanchet, 2022). But one key move is to develop what I call Integrity Checks. It's a simple but powerful process, adapted from Jon Saphier's research (2018). Rather than guessing at how staff perceive our integrity or treating trust as an abstract concept, we work with staff to identify clear actions that show integrity and then use these to get feedback.

1. Illicit characteristics of trust and integrity from your staff.

Begin by having staff respond to this prompt: *I can succeed at my job when I can trust that. . . .*

Have staff work alone first and then process these prompts in groups. Look for them to fill out specific characteristics and actions. For example, Saphier cites common categories like the following:

- *I trust that you will make it safe for us to make mistakes by. . . .*
- *I trust you will show integrity by. . . .*
- *I trust that you think I am a worthwhile person because you. . . .*
- *I trust that you will be honest by. . . .*

2. Develop these characteristics into a survey for feedback.

Flex your Curiosity Mindset by developing what you find into a survey. Turn each category into a Likert scale and provide space for staff to offer one specific thing you can do to best demonstrate this area of integrity and trust. Reflect on the results and look to implement actions that align with the values that move your school forward.

As with openness, we don't know if our integrity is strong unless we both *deliver* actions that align with our values and *accept* feedback on how we can realign.

Affirmation

Last year, I remember seeing a first-year teacher break down in tears. If you've ever mentored or coached a new teacher, you might be thinking, "No surprise, Chase Mielke. Who *doesn't* cry their first years of teaching?" I'm not talking the flavor of "teaching is hard" tears, though. This crying was different—sweet, not salty.

It happened when I gave feedback to Ms. C., a 9th grade teacher who had just graduated a few months prior and was thrust into teaching mid-year. As a part of helping her develop classroom management strategies, we decided to get some perception data: I surveyed groups of students on what they thought was going well and what they hoped Ms. C. could do differently.

I sat down with Ms C. to share the feedback—the trends and the outliers and the ways we could integrate their suggestions appropriately. Like every teacher I've done this with, she expected to get lambasted by student angst. But then I shared this line, spoken by a student and affirmed by many others: *"Ms. C. gives me a reason to actually show up to school."*

Cue leaking eye sockets.

Ms. C. was months into teaching. Every day she came to work, poured her energy into her students, strained and struggled to teach better each day, tried and tried and tried. And this was one of—if not *the*—first affirming comment she had heard.

Affirmation is one of the simplest yet most powerful sources of relatedness. Put simply, we approach good things and avoid bad things. If my organization (or my school leader or my students) don't provide me a source of good, then I'll create as much distance, physically and/or emotionally, as I can. Conversely, I will seek closer connection and commitment to relationships or contexts that make me feel positive, uplifted, supported—or any of the other emotions cued by affirmation. Affirmation is the glue of social connection. It's not surprising, then, that professional recognition serves as a major buffer for cynicism and burnout (Răducu & Stănculescu, 2022).

In our next chapters on efficacy, we'll do a deeper dive into the role of affirmation; it is a critical fuel for *every* worker, so it needs more space than these short few paragraphs. For now, I'll leave you with some reflection questions, followed by a key move:

- How consistently do you share affirmation with your staff? As a group? As individuals?
- How has affirmation (or lack thereof) shaped your career as a school leader? How do your experiences with affirmation shape your actions?
- What are some ways you can provide 5 percent more affirmation to your staff?

Vitamin Supplement: Sticky Note Praise

If affirmation is the glue of social connection, then let's get sticky, using an ingenious little invention called the sticky note. Affirmation is best when it is specific and personalized. But how do we do this when schools are often public spaces? Carry a pad of sticky notes with you everywhere. When you see (or think of) a moment to affirm someone, jot down a quick note and stick it where they can see it.

I first started doing this when students were working independently. Not one to sit at my desk, I decided to circulate and drop little notes to students as they worked. Sometimes these were quick bits of feedback, but more often they were opportunities for quick praise and connection, whether it was a specific note acknowledging a student's performance in the musical or just a general, "I'm glad you're here today." Each note took me a few seconds to write, yet I would watch students beam with smiles and subtly store them in their books or their backpacks for later.

Use the same idea with your staff. As you leave a classroom walk-through, drop a quick positive note on the teacher's desk. Slide one into their mailbox. Place it on their door first thing in the morning. Never let "I forgot" or "I didn't have a way to share this" get in the way of giving people the affirmation they desperately lack yet desperately need.

Listening

With integrity, we focus on our actions, because actions speak louder than words. But there's an irony to this idea: Sometimes the greatest action I can take is to listen—to mute myself so others can be heard. One of the most underestimated practices for building social capital and relatedness is compassionate listening.

Here's the difference between active listening and compassionate listening. Active listening puts our focus on what we are *doing* to show our listening skills. We get in our heads about *our* responses. Compassionate listening, on the other hand, puts the emphasis on understanding another person's experience: What are their struggles, why are they struggling, and what do they need to move forward?

Compassionate listening is, without a doubt, the greatest skill I've learned as an educator, a spouse, and a parent. Though the main space I employ this skill is with school leaders and teachers, I forged it in the difficult context of teaching teenagers.

Teenagers are a tricky group to build social capital for a few reasons:

1. They are sick of being talked at.
2. They often allow you few if any chances to build their trust in you.
3. They are often brimming with angst.

Like a solar eclipse, they open up on their own schedule, give you a limited window, and will burn you if you don't approach them right. I've worked with teenagers for a decade and a half. Through my experiences as a high school teacher—and a peer leadership and listening instructor—I've learned the compassionate listening skills that every leader needs. These skills have transformed my work as a leader, a coach, a parent, a spouse—any role that hinges upon social capital.

To develop compassionate listening, it's as much about what *not* to do rather than what to do.

Vitamin Supplement: Compassionate Listening

Mistake #1: We advise.

This is the hardest habit to cut but the most necessary. Communication isn't only about solving problems. Sometimes it's about processing. For example, a teacher is frustrated with a class, and before they finish their first sentence we hit them with a barrage of advice. *Have you talked to . . . ? You need to. . . . You should try. . . .*

Advice shuts down a person's processing time. It assumes that we know their life better than they do. And, when we interject our advice too soon, we diminish autonomy and destroy dialogue.

Do this instead:

Ask them how they want you to listen. As someone begins to open up, ask them, "How do you want me to listen—do you want me to help you work through a problem or do you want me to just listen right now?"

Ask open-ended questions. One of my students, who frequently came for help through high school (and college), once remarked, "You know what . . . I realized that you barely say anything when I talk to you. You just ask me questions until I figure it out." She became aware of my greatest strategy: the Socratic method. Make it a habit to use questions starting with *what* or *how*.

Rather than saying, "Have you tried pulling that student aside?" try, "What have you already tried? What's working and what isn't?" Most important, root every question in true curiosity. Listen to learn, not to lecture.

Establish a process-to-progress ratio. I anticipate your worry: *If I let people babble on whenever they want, as long as they want, I'll never get anything done. I'm not their counselor!*

When your time is limited, or you want to help people move forward rather than vent, establish a process-to-progress ratio up front. *Process* is the phase where people just put their experience into words and explore their frustration or needs—this is the Curiosity and Compassion phase of being an Illuminating Leader. *Progress* is the Creativity through actions—the phase where we address what we are going to do to move forward. What will we try or do or think differently?

It sounds like this: *"I see you've got a lot on your mind about this. I've got 10 minutes before my next meeting, and I want to give my undivided attention to you right now. How about this: Let's spend five minutes where I'll listen to what's on your mind and then we can dedicate that last five minutes to brainstorming some ideas. Will that work for you?"*

Creating these boundaries ensures clarity, openness, and compassion while protecting our time (and moving toward problem solving).

Mistake #2: We don't acknowledge their experience.

An easy way to miss (or destroy) social capital is when we don't affirm a person's experience. Someone shares a frustration point, and we respond with one of these capital drains like stealing their thunder and making their story about us: *I had that happen before. . . . One time when that happened to me I. . . .* Similar to advising, this mistake is rooted in good intentions. But there's a better way.

Do this instead:

The Feelings-Focused Response. The intentions to share a story about ourselves are noble; we want them to know that we can relate. But there's a better move that is less patronizing and less likely to damage their trust: a feelings-focused response.

Weird name, I know, but it is powerful in its simplicity. The formula is this:

1. Identify the specific emotion a person may be feeling.
2. Wait to confirm if that *is* how they are feeling.
3. Say some variation of, "Tell me more."

You're feeling overwhelmed . . . tell me more about that.
You're feeling devalued . . . let me hear more.
You're angry . . . I'm here to listen.

Seems too easy to work, right? I have a decade of experience show-ing me it does, but the easiest thing you can do is try it. The next time a family or friend is processing something, give it a spin. Two sentences. You have nothing to lose.

Obvious caveat to make sure your nonverbals are sincere and inviting. And, if you're worried—*What if I get the emotion wrong?*—here's what will happen: The person will, without resentment, cor-rect it. *No, it's not that I'm overwhelmed, it's that. . . .* And whether you get the emotion right or they amend it, you'll achieve greater clarity, greater empathy, and greater invitation to build social capital.

Building relatedness isn't only leading with action. It's listening with compassion—genuinely *hearing* a person's needs and working together to alleviate their challenges. Offer your ear, and people will give you their trust.

Each day, our immune system kills cells that could turn into cancer. We bemoan the inevitable school-induced seasonal flu, or we grouch about allergies. But below the surface our immune system battles every minute to help us see another tomorrow.

We empower our physical immune system by giving it what it needs: plenty of water, vitamins, and good sleep. We can't control the fact that our body will experience toxins and viruses throughout the day. But we can build it up to go to battle.

So, too, we must build our school's immune system through related-ness. Support this system with the critical needs of social connection in schools: staff rapport, openness, clarity, integrity, affirmation, and listening. We won't be able to stop every instance of cynicism that creeps into our cultures. But we can ensure that, despite its emergence, our system cannot just function but also flourish.

PART IV

Defeated to Efficacious

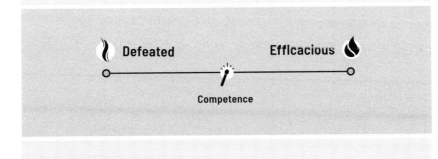

8

Inefficacy 101

When the Twin Towers crumpled under the dust and searing iron of terrorism, Methuselah remained. When millions went to war, killing each other for power and principles and patches of land, Methuselah watched from high and far. When Homer was regaling tails of epic quests, Methuselah sat silent, listening to the whispering winds of time. When coliseums and pyramids and temples rose and crumbled, Methuselah stood firm. Unwavering. Observing. Existing.

Deep within the White Mountains of California, in a secret location among the Ancient Bristlecone Pine Forest, lives Methuselah, one of the oldest trees in the world. Since 2832 BCE, when the Bronze Age was emerging, Methuselah germinated. Now it stands at nearly 208 feet tall, over 4,800 years old—having withstood countless adversities, having survived longer than whole civilizations. Methuselah is a testament of nature's desire for strength, resilience, and growth.

Billions of trees have germinated—some growing, some not. Their survival depends on a lot beyond them: animals and climate and human society. But a tree also survives or thrives from its own abilities. Its bark withstands the weather. Its branches reach for sunlight. Its roots stretch to soak up water and nutrients. And, when these conditions are strong, a tree like Methusclah can withstand change and challenges, hardship and harm. It can do more than only survive. It can thrive.

Like trees, millions of educators have embarked on this career—some staying for decades, others leaving after weeks. Their survival, too, depends on a lot beyond them: their students, the climate of their communities, and the mandates or support of society. But teachers also survive or thrive on their own abilities. Their resilience withstands the adversities of the occupation. Their compassion reaches out to form communities of learners. Their curiosity stretches deep to soak up new talents and skills. And, when these conditions are strong, a teacher—like that one in your building who refuses to retire after 43 years—not only can survive life as an educator but thrive.

Yet, more than ever, teachers are struggling to stand tall like Methuselah. The conditions surrounding them are bringing harsher weather and uprooting their support. Fewer seeds are being planted in education, and those that germinate quickly blow away to new careers in just a handful of years.

As a school leader, much of this change is beyond your control. You don't control the climate of education, nor do you decide how many seeds are sown into education programs. But what is within your influence is the power to ensure that, if a tree lands in your forest, you give it everything it needs to thrive—helping it develop the strength and skill and stability to do this critical work.

In Chapters 8 and 9, we are going to explore the critical role of efficacy, the belief that one has the skills and support necessary to achieve goals. We'll come to understand that, although efficacy is a "feeling" of confidence and optimism, it has concrete effects on teacher well-being, classroom cultures, and student achievement. In understanding its influence on education, we'll also analyze how it develops (or erodes) and how to help educators establish Methuselah-level stability and resilience.

The Years of Uprooting

"I'm on a learning curve because this is my first time having a class of students in person." It took me a few moments to weigh the importance of this sentence, spoken by a first-year teacher I was coaching. It was the fall of 2021, and my colleague's comment brought to surface something I had taken for granted: Student teaching, for many educators in 2020, happened virtually. This teacher's first full-time teaching job was also her first time teaching *in person*.

Later that morning, I met with another colleague in his third year. Within these three years he had taught in person, virtual, hybrid, back to in person, to virtual, and again in person. Along the way he adapted courses to a new learning management system, took on multiple new curricula, and became one of the senior members of his department due to staff retirements and attrition.

In the afternoon, I helped a veteran teacher of over 25 years figure out how to record lessons on video, post them to the virtual course, and brainstorm ways to increase engagement with kids who seemed more addicted than ever to their phones.

Then I capped my day off with a second-career teacher who asked me to explain what terms like *jigsaw* and *formative assessment* meant. She hadn't heard these terms in her last job in the private sector and was yet to learn them in her alternative certification program.

These examples—from one day as an instructional coach—are a microcosm of the experiences challenging educator efficacy across our industry. They are affirmed by the tens of thousands of teachers I've met the past few years on my travels as a speaker and trainer. The years of 2020 and beyond uprooted the efficacy of every educator I've met. The skills, systems, and student needs we *used* to understand became new learning curves—no matter if it was your 1st, your 14th, or your 50th year in education.

Any gardener knows that, when a plant is uprooted, you can't simply shove it back into the ground and expect it to grow well; you must establish and nurture the soil, provide it with nutrients and sun and water—checking on it more often than before. All of this is assuming that the weather conditions haven't changed. But in education, they have. The politics. The pressures. The pure exhaustion of increased workloads and learning curves. We must tend to educator efficacy like a gardener: with care and intention.

Why Efficacy Matters

To understand the importance of efficacy, imagine life without it: *inefficacy*. Actually, you don't need to imagine it because you've seen it in action. A student lacking self-efficacy yields to learned helplessness.

A department without self-efficacy falters and fights when there's a need to try something new. And a teacher without self-efficacy stagnates with skill or doesn't stay a teacher for long.

Self-efficacy is a building block of collective efficacy, which has one of the highest effect sizes on student performance (Hattie, 2008). It is the critical element behind teacher well-being, innovation, engagement, and student performance. High self-efficacy is linked to increased job satisfaction, lower emotional exhaustion, and lower burnout (Skaalvik & Skaalvik, 2016). A teacher's sense of efficacy permeates the educational experience. For example, high levels of self-efficacy in teachers are associated with the following (Leithwood, 2006):

- Decreased tendency to be critical of incorrect responses.
- Increased willingness to work with students experiencing difficulty.
- Development of warm interpersonal relationships in the classroom.
- Promotion of expectations for achievement in the classroom.
- Increased chances of experimenting with instruction.
- Greater willingness to try a variety of materials and approaches.
- Better planning and organization for instruction.
- Higher levels of student achievement across diverse student populations.

Ironically, teachers with high self-efficacy are more likely to seek out support and are more open to coaching. In other words, investing in individual self-efficacy may open the door for more collaboration and collective efficacy. And, as we've already seen how social contagion can increase negative experiences like burnout, social contagion here can work the other way: higher levels of teacher self-efficacy translate to higher levels of student self-efficacy (Ross et al., 2001).

The growth of student performance, then, is nourished by the efficacy of educators. At a time when educational climates seem destined to drought, we still have opportunities to optimize teacher efficacy—adjusting for the things beyond our control by doubling down on what we *can* influence. Thankfully, there is no guesswork needed on how to cultivate teacher efficacy. There are four roots of efficacy that every school leader should know.

The Roots of Efficacy

Who suffers the most from inefficacy? How does it develop—or not? Where should we target our efforts? To start, as my interactions with teachers during the COVID-19 pandemic have revealed, no one is particularly immune to inefficacy. In general, efficacy often follows a curvilinear trend with years of teaching: Self-efficacy increases in early and mid-career but then declines in later stages of a career (Dicke et al., 2014). However, throughout a year, month, classroom, or even day, efficacy can fluctuate because any moment of teaching can yield success or failure (Holzberger et al., 2013).

In Chapter 9, we will explore different strategies for increasing the efficacy of teachers of different experience levels. However, because inefficacy can—and has—affected educators of *all* levels, we should know how efficacy develops in *all* educators.

One of the key researchers of efficacy is a name you know well from your Ed Psych 101 courses in college: Albert Bandura. One of the most influential psychologists of the 20th century, Bandura became interested in self-efficacy while studying the impact of social modeling on alleviating snake phobia (if you're still tense after our ouroboros analogy of micromanagement, read on). He found that one of the major factors in a patient's ability to overcome deeply rooted fears was how they refer to themselves and their abilities.

For decades following his groundbreaking *Social Learning Theory*, he dedicated his energy to understanding the social-cognitive interplay of beliefs, actions, and outcomes. Through this work, he identified the four main roots of efficacy that shape us all.

1. Mastery Experience

In educational spheres, we love to toss around quotes about failure being the fuel of success: *Learn from mistakes! Edison found hundreds of ways how not to make a lightbulb!* Helpful as they are to get that growth mindset grinding, these quotes overlook a critical idea: the greatest source of efficacy is previous success. Any competent teacher knows this inherently. We scaffold our lessons, build standards upon core skills, and "review before new." We do this not because it works for young learners but because building in progressive benchmarks of success works for *all* learners.

This could be why, for example, even veteran teachers experienced inefficacy when schools went virtual to manage COVID-19. Unless they had a lot of previous success with recording lessons, interacting on videoconferences, and developing virtual instruction, teachers had multiple sources of failure all at once. When reflecting on why she left teaching, a friend of mine—who had over 15 years of experience—remarked, "The biggest change for me [teaching throughout the pandemic] was realizing that the strategies and lessons that used to work no longer did."

Although educators may have eventually learned from their mistakes and struggles, they suffered from inefficacy when they felt failure, especially when it affected their students. Failure yields frustration. So, one must have the capacity to first sift through frustration—regulating stress and emotion—before finding future growth (Moss, 2021). (No surprise, then, that an increase in exhaustion predicts an increase in inefficacy.) Success, on the other hand, is a direct source of fuel for efficacy.

We could also use this lens to examine why most professional development is woefully inadequate at shaping actual teaching practice: We "sit and get" new theories in PD but rarely get scaffolded practice, coaching, and feedback to succeed with new implementation. Instead, teachers are often thrown back into their rooms where, upon failing at implementing a new (raw) practice or theory, they quickly revert to the strategies they think have worked better in the past. Or, teachers get so overwhelmed with a massive overhaul of change from a new initiative that they aren't able to implement or experience small steps of success.

Mastery experience is *the* most important root of efficacy. Every move we make as school leaders—whether it is aimed at helping parents, students, or staff—should be framed around this question: How do we build pathways of increasing success from the introduction of an idea through the mastery of a skill?

2. Social Modeling (Vicarious Experience)

If learning from our own successes is the strongest root of efficacy, learning from others comes second. The ability to observe another person's actions—and mirror or imitate them—is one of the core skills that allows humans to advance individually and collectively. A baby learns to clap by watching someone else clap. A child learns to climb monkey bars by watching other kids first. Students learn speech and sentence patterns by hearing and seeing them in others. A teacher learns how to implement Socratic seminars by seeing videos, scripts, or peers in action. Sure, any one of these could be learned *without* seeing them modeled first, but the rate of efficacy and success increases relative to the amount of social modeling.

Educational training follows an apprenticeship model for a reason; teachers-in-training traditionally observe mentors for hours and months before control is slowly released to them. Observing masterful teaching helps preservice teachers see theories put into action, forming a base of understanding what works. Unfortunately, after preservice teaching, education often suffers from teachers working in silos. We get thrown to the wolves without the time, agency, incentive, or support to observe other teacher practices, thus missing a major source of efficacy.

Another challenge of social modeling is vicarious failure. Just as we can build efficacy by seeing another succeed, we can erode efficacy by observing someone fail. If my fellow human falls through a trap on a path, it's easier to avoid that path than to conquer it. In education it looks like this: We observe another teacher try a new strategy and, if it doesn't succeed, we quickly dismiss the strategy as ineffective. Conscientious observers—and those subscribing to "failure is feedback!" adages—might take the time and energy to analyze *why* it didn't work. However, most educators default to "I'll spare myself the time (which I don't have a lot of) and the trouble of failing like they did. I'll avoid that strategy."

The silver lining of education today is the unprecedented number of resources available to help teachers learn vicariously. There are more videos, blogs, and virtual courses of effective teaching practices at the fingertips of educators than at any time in human history. Still, if we want educators to leverage social modeling, we must ensure that time, encouragement, and targeted support are a default part of developing educator efficacy.

3. Verbal Persuasion

"I don't understand where you were going with that lesson." A dagger of disappointment struck my poor little student-teacher heart when my mentor teacher said this to me following my first solo lesson. It was painful. Not only had I felt like my lesson failed—I *knew* it failed from this feedback from Sherry, a veteran teacher of over 30 years.

Verbal persuasion is another way of saying "feedback." Verbal persuasion can be constructive or destructive. Pleasant or painful. Timely or delayed. The feedback I got from Sherry was timely—right after the lesson. It was painful. But, despite the pain, the conversation that followed was one of the most constructive experiences for my budding educator efficacy.

I've come to learn that mastery experience is not simply the most important source of efficacy; it is *the* source of efficacy. Consider the other three sources (social modeling, verbal persuasion, and emotional/physical states) as supports for mastery experience. Social modeling only works if it models mastery experience. Verbal persuasion only works if it provides feedback toward mastery experience. And positive emotional and physical states only work if they motivate us toward mastery experience.

Which is why, despite the pain of failing a lesson, Sherry's verbal persuasion was so helpful. Upon my failure—which was to add a video because it would be "fun"—Sherry helped me analyze the lesson design around *effectiveness*. She gave me tangible steps to take when planning the next lesson with intentionality. And the feedback worked.

This is a critical distinction: We don't give verbal persuasion to make people *feel better*. We provide verbal persuasion that leads toward greater mastery experience. "Great job on that lesson" isn't as powerful as "Great job adapting that lesson using formative feedback—your flexibility helped your students grow." The former boosts moods, but the latter boosts mastery experience.

Verbal persuasion as an extension of mastery experience also emphasizes credibility. The more we see the feedback provider as credible, the more it affects our efficacy (Pfitzner-Eden, 2016). The feedback of others—peers, students, parents, administrators—influences us to the degree that we think these people know (and can show) what they are talking about. I clung to every word Sherry gave me, not because I had to, but because she was a multi-decade master teacher.

Verbal persuasion can be a powerful way to enhance efficacy. But we must be intentional. We must have the credibility to give feedback (or outsource to those who do). And, we must ensure that the words we use help people toward mastery and action, not just mood and attitude.

4. Emotional and Physiological States

A caveat to the last section on verbal persuasion: Although verbal feedback should be aimed at mastery experience, not every sentence we speak to others should be verbal feedback. It is OK, using praise or affirmation, to help people feel positive emotion. Not only is it *OK* to cultivate positive emotion—when it comes to efficacy, positive emotion can be critical.

In 1953, psychologists Peter Milner and James Olds stumbled upon the brain's reward circuit. By using electrodes to stimulate the septum in the brains of rats, they could give rats a hit of dopamine whenever they chose. Within minutes they could "train" rats to go to a particular corner of a box, simply by giving their brains hits of dopamine. When they gave rats a lever to stimulate their own reward circuit, rats would hit the lever up to 100 times every minute (Linden, 2012). Rats would abandon their nursing babies, cross electrified floors, and skip sex and food to get hits of dopamine. Without researchers intervening, starving rats would choose the lever—the hits of positive emotion—rather than eat a meal to stay alive. They would choose dopamine to the point of death.

Why does this matter? Because it illustrates a critical point: The purpose of positive emotion isn't to *feel* good. Positive emotion drives motivation. Our motivational systems, simmered to their essence, hinge upon two decisions: approach treats or avoid threats. If a choice doesn't help me avoid a threat—even a psychological one—or lead me toward a treat—even a psychological one—then I won't do it.

Therefore, feeling pleasant emotion (or avoiding unpleasant emotion) is a fuel of efficacy. Having noticeable, measurable moments of success function like a rat's dopamine lever. Success releases dopamine, which drives motivation, which increases effort and practice, which fuels more success. When we help people feel affirmed, praised, or empowered, we are becoming better (legal) dopamine dealers. We are fueling self-efficacy.

Conversely, unpleasant emotions can damage self-efficacy. For example, we often fall into cognitive distortions like emotional reasoning, where we equate how we *feel* to how we *are*. A teacher may feel a sense of failure because a lesson didn't go well and equate feeling failure to *being* a failure. An administrator may attempt to motivate a teacher, saying, "That lesson wasn't good enough," only to lead a teacher to think, "*I* am not good enough." In my experience, teachers are particularly susceptible to this negative emotional reasoning because we often tie our efficacy as teachers to our identity as people. For this reason, we should leverage our Curiosity and Compassion Mindsets when we know people have felt frustration.

Efficacy researchers also highlight the importance of *physiological* states and not just emotional. Our minds are connected to somatic indicators—often subconscious checks of our physical state, energy, and mood. If I sweat or my heart rate increases, I might mistake that rise response as a flaw—I become anxious because I think my body is telling me I'm not good enough (Pfitzner-Eden, 2016). It is also harder, for example, to feel efficacious when we're stressed or tired. While we can't control whether a teacher has great sleep hygiene, exercise habits, or dietary choices, we can take action on reducing exhaustion and stress—as we explored in Chapters 3 and 4.

"Feeling good," whether physiologically or emotionally, isn't only a by-product of efficacy; it's the fuel that drives it.

The Virus: Lack of Recognition

The importance of verbal persuasion and positive emotional states reveal how one burnout virus, lack of recognition, can negatively affect self-efficacy. A 2017 Gallup poll found that only 29 percent of teachers received recognition or praise for doing good work in the last week (Hodges, 2022). Juxtapose that with findings that teachers who receive regular praise are more productive, more engaged at work, more likely to stay with their school, and more likely to receive higher satisfaction scores from students and parents. Sure, we get that one day a year of forced recognition via Teacher Appreciation Day. And maybe we get an occasional email from a parent or former student.

But these occasional moments of recognition are like the rainfall of a desert. Perhaps they will yield a temporary boost of verdant life, but the lushness doesn't linger as droughts dictate the landscape. Therefore, without *frequent* positive emotion and verbal persuasion—encouragement, affirmation, recognition, and support—our efforts to bolster retention and reduce burnout will fail.

Studies bear this out, with one study of over 7,000 workers finding that lack of appreciation is strongly linked to *each* dimension of burnout: exhaustion, cynicism, and inefficacy. For example, compared to workers who feel appreciated,

- Twice as many underappreciated workers feel overburdened by work.
- Three times as many underappreciated workers would quit their jobs if they could.
- Three times as many underappreciated workers feel they can't handle their job tasks effectively.
- Four times as many underappreciated workers feel alienated from their work or colleagues.
- Four times as many underappreciated workers feel that their boss expects too much of them.

The authors of the study write that "The only thing worse than undervaluing the importance of appreciation is underestimating the consequences of a lack of it" (Jerabek, 2018, para. 4). Positive recognition is the sunlight and water that does more than just grow the roots of efficacy; it creates conditions where educators can grow strong, withstanding the winds of exhaustion and cynicism and failure—rising tall and empowered to bear the fruits of student learning and growth. The question is, are you watering the roots of your team enough?

Your Crops Need You

Your team *wants* to grow. Remember that. No educator, staff member, or student seeks stagnation. We are all wired to grow—to learn and advance and succeed. Although every seed is different, our work conditions exhibit great influence on our growth. Will we find the soil of our culture barren and rocky, impenetrable for the roots of our efficacy? Or will we find it rich with resources and space to spread? Will our leaders plant us where positive sunlight permeates? Will they water us with affirmation and recognition for the hard work of bearing fruit despite the climate changes of education? Or will we suffer and struggle to suck up enough energy and fuel before the winds of adversity whip us away?

The ultimate factor in the growth of your team is you, the person reading this book. You, the school leader, have the greatest influence on efficacy. You create the systems, cultivate the cultures, and tend to the needs of your staff like no one else can. You are capable of creating educational Methuselahs. So, let's get growing.

9

Competence

Let's turn our analogy from nourishing tree seeds to different seeds: tiny humans.

Maybe, dear reader, you've decided like my wife and I to raise one of these tiny humans. Maybe, also like my wife and I, questioning our sanity, you've decided to raise more than one of them. Or maybe you've decided that, instead of having children, you'd have things like quality sleep, free time, and disposable income. Regardless of your direct experience with these creatures, try to picture a baby when they're freshly born (don't picture too vividly . . . it's gross). What are the core skills that the average baby comes with pre-equipped?

Here's a quick list:

- Digesting
- Breathing
- Sound making (sweet sounds like cooing and dagger-to-your-ear-hole sounds like crying)
- Basic senses (although some, like vision, are pretty rough)
- A few reflexes

And that's about it. Pretty terrible résumé and no real employable skills. But one thing we often miss from this list is our *most* important skill: risk taking.

Let's fast forward our sample baby's life to a moment of risk-taking skill in action: the moment a child learns to walk. This scene fascinates me because—no matter who the parents are—it looks the same.

After many, many risks and efforts, our tiny human gets the skill of standing. At a certain point, this vertical stability is not enough to satisfy said tiny human. Risks must be taken! Tiny baby, wobbling as they hold onto something, sets their eyes on something distant, looking woozy. Parents, drawing upon a sixth sense, realize a key moment is upon them. Yawping commences as parents scramble for a phone (*Hit record! No, a video! Not a picture! You're taking a picture!*). Our woozy wobbler takes the risk, raises the chubby leg, lands the fat foot—and smashes their whole body to the floor.

Parents swoop in to scoop our child prodigy off the floor, clapping, celebrating, debating which Ivy League T-shirt to buy. And the baby, despite losing the battle royale of gravity and ground, despite even shedding real tears, rises again, ready for another round.

This practice happens over and over, each time the baby takes literal *baby steps* of efficacy. It is through this innate wiring—the desire to take risks—that walking becomes a skill. Why does this matter for us?

First, let's notice what is absent from the scene. The baby is not scolded or condemned for the failure. No one rates the baby a C– because they took longer to walk than a sibling. No one slides the baby a rubric saying, "Minimally effective." Risk—even resulting in failure— is celebrated, cherished, and rewarded.

Second, we must consider this fact: there is no growth without risk. We do not develop skill unless we step beyond comfort and into discomfort. This requirement does not change as we get older. Whether it's learning Polish or piano or project-based learning, we must take risks to grow.

This leads to our critical question of this chapter: How do we better encourage, honor, and support the risk taking of our educators to build their efficacy?

The Efficacy Ladder

Here we have a conundrum. We know that we must take risky steps to grow. But risk is stressful, and education is already stressful as is, sometimes overwhelmingly so. Although we are innately wired to take risks, life experience—and the culture surrounding risk—often erodes our efficacy-inducing impulses. A baby failing to walk is celebrated. A teacher failing in front of students is criticized—sometimes openly from students or administration. We saw in Chapter 3 that, when stress levels become high, rather than taking risks, we withdraw, protecting ourselves as much as possible. Therefore, we are challenged to help educators embrace the stress of risk taking in an already stressful occupation. We must create cultures where risk is promoted and pressure is reduced.

Here's how we step our efficacy-building cultures up to another level (pun enjoyably intended). The most powerful model I've used to do this is what I call the Efficacy Ladder. The concept is simple, but the application is powerful. I first used this framework to help struggling students make academic gains—often catalyzing them to go from failing grades to content efficacy. I now use this ladder anytime I can, whether it's personal goals like writing this book, helping teachers I coach develop instructional efficacy, or helping my former district plan the effective rollout of new initiatives. Here's how it works:

Imagine a ladder (see Figure 9.1). At the top of that ladder is the end goal, like running a marathon or writing an effective essay or implementing whole-school cross-curricular writing. Then, running down the rungs of the ladder is each preceding step that must be accomplished *before* the previous. So, before I can run 26.2 miles, I should probably be able to run at least 20. Before 20 miles, I should probably be able to run at least 15. And so on. Depending on the top-level goal, there might be *many* rungs or a few. At the bottom is something critical: an easy goal that can be accomplished in the next 48 hours to make progress toward efficacy (e.g., getting off the couch and running to the end of my street and back)

The structure of this ladder does several things. First, it makes the end goal clear. Second, it breaks the big goal into understandable substeps—steps that can allow us to realistically understand the time and effort it will take. Last, and I'd argue most important, it provides us a simple goal that we can take immediate action on—one that is manageable enough to encourage our first risk yet simple enough to give us the dopamine boost we need to fuel future motivation.

Let's look at an example for a teacher. Maybe I want to leverage Socratic circles to increase student discussion: my end goal. But my

FIGURE 9.1

The Efficacy Ladder

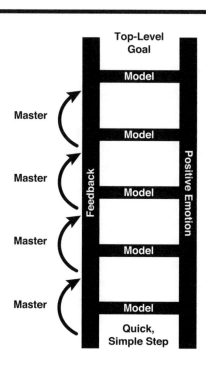

class can't go five seconds without interrupting one another. With my end goal established, I work backward, realizing that, before they can do Socratic discussions, they need to have structures for responding to one another. Before they can use these structures with complex content, they must use them in simple conversation. And, before they can do this in conversation, they would benefit from being able to do this in writing—exchanging responses with one another, using pretaught discussion structures. Before I can even *get* them to do these written responses, I have to be vigilant that "silent writing time" is in fact silent so they can focus. With my ladder set, I realize that my priority goal over the next week is being overt, clear, and consistent with silent writing time for students to explore ideas. Although silent writing seems a long leap away from animated Socratic discussions, my goal has intentionality: I have a small step I can achieve that (a) gives me a hit of dopamine as I achieve success and (b) makes the next step easier, working toward a top-level goal. Mastery experience coupled with positive emotional states.

Leaders can use growth ladders to grow more than just classroom efficacy. Before rolling out a new initiative, establish what the end goal is. Then, work backward, setting substeps. Look at the steps realistically. How long will it take to achieve efficacy with this initiative? What are the immediate steps that we must master before we move up the ladder of efficacy? What structures and supports are we building into our professional development and schedule to ensure these immediate steps are reached?

Notice how this ladder is strategically built to engage *mastery experience*, our most important root of efficacy. Every small success yields the mastery we need. It's also designed to cue *positive emotional states*, our second root, as we accomplish these steps. But let's take this efficacy ladder to new heights (I know, I need to chill with the puns).

Between each rung, we maximize efficacy growth by building in *social modeling*. In our Socratic discussion example, students will gain efficacy faster if the teacher models success at each step. *What sentence stems will encourage thoughtful discussion? What does an effective written response look like? What does the teacher mean by "silent writing"?* Each step provides a perfect opportunity to model.

Last, along the entire experience, represented by the poles of the ladder, should be *verbal persuasion*: frequent, ongoing feedback, affirmation, and praise. How do we ensure that educators know whether the step they took worked? How do we give them strategies and suggestions if they aren't advancing? And how do we praise them for their effort, despite success or failure?

We know that feedback is most effective when it is timely, specific, and provides strategies of what to do differently. Yet consider how the feedback the average teacher receives is devoid of these three things. Sure, they might get instant feedback that a lesson fails when students are confused, frustrated, or bouncing off the walls. But this feedback rarely suggests what to do differently. Or, a teacher may have an administrator observe them a couple times a year. Then, they may wait days—or months—before receiving feedback (often in sparse, written comments rather than in-person dialogue) on their lesson. Sometimes the feedback is simply a rubric score; teachers are lucky if the feedback provides tangible, context-appropriate strategies. The Efficacy Ladder urges us to provide the timely, specific, and actionable feedback educators need to grow.

When we think about building a teacher's competence using the Efficacy Ladder, we provide each of the four roots of efficacy. We intentionally and strategically embed these roots into our actions and cultures. We stoke the innate fire of a person's desire to take risks.

Impressionable Puppies and Teaching Old Dogs New Efficacy

Is efficacy developed the same way for a veteran teacher as a novice? Do we change our strategy for support depending on a teacher's experience? No matter the person, efficacy still has four major roots: mastery experience, social modeling, verbal persuasion, and positive emotional and physical states. However, studies comparing experience levels show differences worth noting.

First, a disclaimer: Efficacy is context dependent. Having efficacy in one context doesn't automatically translate to a new context. I have strong efficacy teaching high schoolers. Although many of my teaching skills are strong, if I were thrown into teaching 2nd grade, I'd be in for a world of hurt (and laughs from my wife) due to the learning curve. Thus, anytime a teacher shifts contexts—a new content area, new grade level, new school, new anything—we must be mindful that their efficacy is in flux.

Generally, though, as teachers gain years of experience, their efficacy strengthens. One study found that veteran teachers scored higher on efficacy for classroom management and instructional strategies (Tschannen-Moran & Hoy, 2007). However, engagement scores were the same as novice teachers (e.g., using a new piece of technology may "level the field"). This same study found that context (e.g., urban, suburban, rural) and demographics (e.g., race, gender) did *not* account for significant variance of efficacy.

No matter the teacher, mastery experience is still our greatest asset. Veteran teachers can gain efficacy faster, in part, because they have more past mastery experience to draw upon when teaching gets difficult. Verbal persuasion is also less effective for veteran teachers as their barometer of success is their own judgment versus an external observer.

Should we change our approach, then, to efficacy support based on experience level? Yes and no. Despite the differences, our core strategies for building educator efficacy should be the same. But increasing the frequency and intensity of these strategies is critical any time a teacher switches contexts. Young puppies are particularly susceptible to shifts in efficacy. But that doesn't mean our old dogs don't need support and attention too.

The Big Three

One of the most flattering comments I ever heard about teaching was from my good friend who is a nuclear engineer. I can't begin to imagine the complexity of a nuclear engineer's job. Yet one time, after he was tasked with teaching and training other nuclear engineers for a week, he said, "I have no idea how you do your job as a teacher. I have never been so mentally drained and tired after a day of work, doing what you do. You have to be *on* constantly." All right, it would be cool to get an engineer's level of pay for this complex work we do. But hearing an absurdly intelligent "outsider" speak with respect toward our profession reminded me how complex this work is. We must build efficacy with *so* many things beyond standing and talking—technology, communication, content expertise, posting assignments on learning management systems, establishing clarity on IEPs, explaining the nuance and rhetorical advantages of active versus passive construction. Where do we start to build efficacy when there are *so* many things that require efficacy?

Just as a few core subatomic particles—protons, neutrons, and electrons—shape life as we know it, there are three core things that shape teaching: classroom management, assessment/feedback, and instruction. We should invest our time on climbing these "big three" efficacy ladders that demand the most time and energy—and have a huge influence on student learning. This isn't to say that we *shouldn't* give ample time to coaching teachers on using a new learning management system, for example; every initiative should be coupled with a commitment to supporting staff efficacy (and planned using an Efficacy Ladder). But these big three represent our largest payoff. One analysis found that, of the six major factors underpinning teacher efficacy, five of them were directly related to instruction, management, and/or assessment (Skaalvik & Skaalvik, 2007). Efficacy with the big three is critical because they most influence burnout, retention, and student performance. To help you apply a Compass and Curiosity Mindset, see Appendix C for a sample survey to assess efficacy in these big three.

Classroom management, for instance, has the biggest influence on burnout according to one metanalysis (Ozdemir, 2007). And struggles with classroom management affected all three dimensions of burnout. Any educator can understand this relationship. In 2016, when I nearly left education, my biggest stressor was my highly rebellious second period. Not only did my stress levels rise before, during, and after that class (the mention of specific names, years later, still send residual twitches of angst up my spine), but my struggles with them also increased my cynicism. I felt myself caught in a spiral of trying a new strategy, watching it fail (inefficacy), getting frustrated at students (cynicism), and being drained as the cycle spun anew every day (emotional exhaustion). We know that classroom management is a keystone of powerful teaching, but it's also the keystone of retaining teachers.

Feedback/assessment is another area with huge implications for efficacy and performance. Teachers amass a lot of time, even beyond contractual hours, sifting through student work, assessing progress, providing feedback, and tailoring instruction. Picture, for example, the learning erosion that occurs when a teacher lacks competence or efficacy with feedback and assessment. Students get delayed (thus less effective) feedback, hampering their growth and spurring frustration as learners. Student work piles up on a teacher's to-do list, leading to exhaustion and rushed responses. Inefficacy with adapting instruction to assessment yields "covered content" without true learning.

Classroom management, feedback/assessment, and instruction are the most worthwhile areas for efficacy support. With these big three in mind, here are some important strategies school leaders can implement to help teachers climb efficacy ladders.

Spotter Ready? The Role of Coaching

It was only a matter of time until the importance of coaching found its place in this book. Coaches are among the most powerful change agents of efficacy, whether it's a soccer coach, my son's piano teacher, or an instructional coach at school. Coaching is significant because it often utilizes all four roots of efficacy. Typically, a coach helps a teacher work incrementally toward an established goal, creating mastery experiences. Strategies are often demonstrated, using social modeling. Conversations and feedback provide verbal persuasion and, if the coach is effective, the experience can provide positive emotions of affirmation, joy, and relatedness. Studies on efficacy confirm this finding, with one review of research noting, "The greater the opportunity for collaboration with other adults and the more observations that were made, the greater the resulting sense of efficacy" (Tschannen-Moran & Hoy, 2007). If coaching is so powerful, then, why don't *all* teachers receive coaching *all* the time?

Here's the thing: In many school districts, "coaching" is a four-letter word (and not one of the fun ones). I've lost count of how many times teachers have approached me after a workshop or training to lament how they were forced by a school leader to have a coach work with them after a bad evaluation. Their criticism of coaching mirrors my experience being on the other end as a coach. I had to work tirelessly to help teachers shift their perception and not see coaching as either intrusive or insulting. Before talking about strategies for using coaching to build efficacy, let's chat about why coaching often fails and how to ensure it succeeds.

At its core, coaching fails to be effective—fails to influence efficacy—when it is at odds with the central ideas of this book.

Coaching Fails When Teachers Don't Have Agency

When teachers are forced to receive coaching, agency gets lost. This is particularly problematic when required coaching is coupled with evaluation processes. Tying coaching to evaluations often becomes a game to play. A teacher who is forced to have a coach after a bad evaluation often has high stress levels of being "under the gun" coupled with low efficacy of feeling criticized and incompetent. If teachers don't have agency to what, why, and how they are coached, the experience often fails to fuel efficacy. To get the best results out of coaching, make it nonevaluative and teacher-initiated whenever and however possible (we'll look at some ideas on this soon).

Coaching Fails When Teachers Are Too Exhausted and Overworked

Coaching takes time. Teachers need to set specific goals, collect data on these goals, review the data and get feedback, brainstorm new approaches, plan for those approaches, and attempt them (thus, starting a new cycle). Doing this work during planning periods or after school adds exhaustion and "kicks the can" of other work down the road. Pulling teachers out of class to observe another class requires subplans (more work) and the stress of being out of class. Coaching shouldn't be an add-on. It should be infused with a teacher's existing workload. If these are your only options to make coaching work in your district, then work extra hard to ensure that other workloads are reduced.

Coaching Fails When Coaches Aren't Skilled at Building Relatedness

Although I've often heard people promote coaching in schools with "Even elite athletes still have coaches!" there are some major differences between coaching an athlete and coaching a teacher. Beyond the obvious salary differences, athletes are used to their work being public for all to see. Teachers aren't. Many teachers are highly private about their practice, often nervous to fail in front of others or be authentic for fear of judgment. They are also often overworked and cynical of consultants who aren't living their world. For example, the less a teacher identifies with the person they observe—even if that person is highly successful—the less likely the social modeling or verbal persuasion increases the observer's efficacy (Tschannen-Moran & Hoy, 2007). For these and many other reasons, coaches must be highly skilled at developing trusting relationships with those they coach. Without trust and warmth, coaches—even those who were exceptional teachers—can struggle to make an impact on educator efficacy.

Coaching can be our greatest support for growing efficacy. But it *must* consider everything else this book has promoted: reduced workloads, teacher agency, and trust. Take some time to evaluate how well your school is honoring these needs. Better yet, adopt a Curiosity Mindset and get feedback from your staff on their coaching experience and how to improve it.

Coaching Strategies

Coaching is a beast, and there are robust resources beyond this book to help your school tame this beast and wield its power to build educator efficacy. I'll at least mention that, in my 15 years, out of the *many* models of coaching I've experienced as a teacher and coach, Jim Knight's *Impact Cycle* (2017)—and all the work from Instructional Coaching Institute—has been the most effective I've seen and used, in large part because Knight's methodology and Partnership Principles are built to foster educator agency in the coaching process.

Not every school's coaching approach is equal. Some build coaching into every teacher's day. Other teachers rarely, if ever, receive coaching support. Some schools have designated full-time roles, and others don't. Considering these disparities, I want to offer up a few suggestions that any school district can use to give effective feedback and support educator efficacy. These strategies can be either combined with existing coaching models or used as a starting point for boosting educator efficacy.

Strategy #1: Objective Feedback as the DIY Coach

Although I mentioned earlier that coaching a teacher is, in some ways, different from coaching an athlete, there is one area where teachers *should* be coached like athletes: the use of objective data. Much of traditional coaching involves observers giving their opinions on a teacher's practice—reflections often riddled with subjectivity and bias. Elite athletes don't get feedback on what their coaches "think" happened; they get precise, objective data. Sports statisticians break down their performance into microseconds and quantified touches and "phases of play." They pore over video in slow motion to watch the flex of a muscle or frame of the opponent's positioning.

OK, we don't have designated statisticians for every classroom or the fancy equipment (or time) to capture every frame of interaction. But we can emulate an athlete's effort to get objective with data—far beyond standardized test scores. Empower teachers with DIY coaching by looking at objective data of their interactions with students.

Video recording is one of the easiest ways. Watching our own instruction is one of the most objective pieces of evidence we have—we see what we actually say and what students actually do rather than how we remember the lesson. We may find out, as I have, that we talk way more than we think, which encourages us to look for ways to shift the ratio of interaction. We may find that we call on the same few students even though we remembered having a wider pool of responses. Or we may find that the lesson we thought went horribly wrong was actually pretty effective, thus boosting our efficacy via positive emotion.

Video is convenient because every teacher I know has access to a camera—either through their school or in their palms with their smartphone. And, although it is helpful to watch the video with a master teacher who can foster deeper reflection, watching ourselves solo still yields ample feedback for improving efficacy, especially if you couple it with the intra-coaching strategy I describe below.

Beyond video, there are other emerging ways to get objective feedback today. With my former district, for example, we started using the software TeachFX. Teachers or coaches audio-record a lesson and then run the recording through TeachFX to get a detailed report the next day of things like the following:

- Teacher versus student talk time.
- Frequency and diversity of student responses.
- Frequency and duration of think time.
- Number of times a teacher builds off student contributions.
- Transcription of the entire lesson.
- Word clouds of frequent words to note key vocabulary.

These reports provide objective measures that can be used for setting individual or group goals around engagement and student interaction. This is an example of how we can use technology to reduce the subjectivity of coaching and empower teachers to source their own feedback.

Last, consider using DIY coaching to reduce workloads. Rather than another formal observation from an administrator, a teacher records a lesson and reflects on their performance alongside their administrator. Not only does this provide far more impactful, objective, and relevant feedback, but it creates flexibility and a reduction of both the administrator's *and* the teacher's workloads as a substitution, rather than an additional task.

Strategy #2: Intra-Coaching

While watching a video of a lesson can be a great source of feedback for building efficacy, having more targeted reflections can bolster efforts to grow. As you work toward boosting efficacy in an area, develop key questions educators can use for more intentional reflection.

Below is a list of some of my favorites, adapted from Jim Knight's coaching questions (Knight, 2017):

1. On a scale of 1–10 (1 being worst ever, 10 being best ever), how would you rate that lesson?
2. Why did you give it that rating?
3. What went well?
4. What would students have done differently to boost it a point or two?
5. What evidence would you look for to see that students are doing _____ differently?
6. What strategy could you try tomorrow or next week to help students _____?
7. What support would you need to try this strategy?

Each question has a purpose. Some help a teacher focus on the good to cue positive emotional states. Others prompt for specific steps to encourage mastery experience. And the last question helps identify supports like feedback or social modeling that school leaders can help provide.

Strategy #3: Inter-Coaching

"The most beneficial thing we ever did was watch other teachers." My wife remarked this when we were chatting about our district's coaching strategies. Even as a veteran teacher, she found much more benefit in watching another teacher's strategies and approaches versus having a coach tell her how she taught. Remember: social modeling is a major root of efficacy. Harness it by building in systems for teachers to learn from one another.

One often untapped space for this is using team meetings or PLCs to help teachers build individual and collective efficacy. While we might *think* that teams are doing an in-depth conversation of skills and strategies, oftentimes this isn't the case. In Chapter 4, we explored that data meetings often miss the mark because they often

- Discuss data that isn't chosen by or relevant to teachers (i.e., they are micromanaged).
- Force teachers to focus on surface-level solutions (such as a worksheet design or excusing student behavior) because real solutions take more time than teachers are given to implement.
- Are too short or meet too infrequently to make a difference.

My personal experience confirms this research as team meetings are often devoid of (a) the time necessary to create change and (b) the opportunity to actually watch one another teach. Team meetings, though, can present a powerful space to help build efficacy if used well. Here are some ideas to help:

- **Ask your teachers** how their current team meetings could be more helpful for building their efficacy. Listen and implement their answers. I can't overstate this point: Research by Ross and Gray (2006) found major boosts to efficacy when principals provided individualized support, fostered trust and mutual respect, problem solved with teachers, and listened to their needs.

- **Dedicate *ample* time to this work.** Frequency and length of time matter—make sure the inertia of "getting started" doesn't erode so much time that nothing gets accomplished. Either meet frequently enough to not lose steam or provide large, dedicated time blocks (see Figure 9.2).
- **Utilize video.** Rather than pulling teachers from classes to observe one another, have them record themselves and review selected chunks in pairs or groups.
- **Implement microteaching models,** which place teachers in low-risk scenarios with colleagues to practice specific skills and gain valuable feedback before trying them with students.
- **Revisit a commitment to value practices over programs** (see Chapter 4). Implementing new programs can trigger inefficacy as they must be "adopted," suggesting (and often requiring) massive time commitments and learning curves. Practices, on the other hand, are "adapted"—we often have some level of efficacy with key practices already. Invest time and money into PD that allows colleagues to work together and develop group mastery over key practices rather than large scale programs.

Strategy #4: Grow-Your-Own PD Tracks

Let's flip back to sports for a moment and imagine a soccer team. At practice one day, the coaching staff decides to focus on shooting. Six hours are dedicated to getting the whole team to improve their shooting abilities. Defenders practice shooting. The goalie practices shooting. Even the players who are exceptional at shooting—the ones who could really improve their passing game—also practice shooting. One would argue that, even though shooting is a critical skill in soccer, this approach to training is *far* from the most efficient use of time. Unique roles have unique needs for efficacy growth.

But this is what traditional PD looks like in too many schools. An entire staff goes through the same PD, whether it applies to them or not (shout-out to specials teachers here) or whether this is actually a skill they need (and let's be honest, if it were a school PD, they would spend more time talking about the "theory of shooting" than actually, y'know, shooting).

FIGURE 9.2

How Much Time Is Needed?

Time is one of the scarcest resources in education. As such, whenever I bring up the importance of coaching for boosting efficacy, school leaders often ask, "How much time is needed?" The answer depends on a number of factors:

- Do you have designated coaching positions?
- Are teachers using intra-coaching methods?
- Are they inter-coaching in pairs or in groups?
- Do teachers already have designated time blocks to be coached, or are coaching conversations happening before or after school?

However, the key to getting results is to ensure educators have enough time to complete full coaching cycles. Typically, a coaching cycle involves

1. Establishing a baseline of data/observation.
2. Identifying an area to improve.
3. Researching/learning a new strategy to improve the targeted area.
4. Experimenting with the new strategy and collecting another round of data.
5. Getting feedback (comparing data, reflecting on what worked and what didn't, identifying next steps, etc.).

If there isn't enough time provided to complete full cycles, then coaching likely won't make much impact (and will feel like a waste of time to teachers *because* it doesn't make much impact).

Each school is unique in the commitment it can provide to coaching, but there are basically two approaches:

The Burst Approach: Providing enough time in one chunk so a complete cycle can occur

A great example of using the Burst Approach is microteaching, which has a high effect size on student achievement. Typically, teachers plan and practice a new strategy in a small group, sometimes even just in front of their peers as a "mock lesson." Peers or observers provide feedback after the mock lesson. Using a half-day or a full day of PD is a reasonable chunk of time for implementing microteaching.

FIGURE 9.2

How Much Time Is Needed? (Continued)

The Block Approach: Setting aside frequent, small blocks of time to complete the different steps of a coaching cycle

Most schools attempt the block approach. For example, on one day a teacher does a preconference with a coach to establish a plan and discuss strategies. Another day, the coach observes a teacher's lesson. Then, another day they reflect on the observation together.

The closer these blocks occur together, the more effective. I've seen some schools go weeks between these blocks, at which point they are often ineffective as feedback isn't timely. I've seen other schools do blocks effectively by using designated, weekly inter-coaching. For example, teams or departments meet one week to establish strategies to experiment with that week, then they collect data/recordings to discuss at the next week's meeting.

Although there isn't a "golden schedule" of coaching that fits for every school, if coaching is worth doing (and it is), it's worth planning so that teachers get full cycles of support and feedback.

In Chapter 4, we explored the value of giving teachers agency in PD. Here, it makes return as not just a way to increase autonomy but to support teacher efficacy. A school can still have a unified focus—still work toward common goals; however, a unified focus isn't an "all-or-nothing" approach to PD. Options can still apply. One of the best concepts for this is microcredentialing.

You may be familiar with microcredentialing: Teachers have options for developing skills in specific areas. Working through a process, they earn recognized credentials within the district. Approaches to microcredentials vary in education, but experts agree that they have these essential components (Carbaugh et al., 2022):

1. Clear learning targets.
2. Success criteria (which will also be found in the rubric).
3. Resources to learn about and prepare for the learning task.
4. Job-embedded activities designed to demonstrate the learning targets (such as a performance task).

5. A pre-reflection to activate prior knowledge and provide context for the task and a post-reflection to consider the impact of the performance task on teacher practice and student outcomes.
6. A description of the evidence that will be used to assess competency.

The first thing to note with these components is that they run parallel with efficacy ladders: clear end goals, structured substeps, ample feedback, and support. There are other reasons microcredentialing is threatening to disrupt the $8 billion PD industry. First, it still allows school leaders to have a unified focus with the sort of credentials on which a teacher can build efficacy. Second, it provides teachers choice in their PD—they can choose a route they most need or feel passionate about. It is also affirming to educators; they get real recognition and progress once they have demonstrated mastery. For schools that *really* want to support positive working conditions, achieving mastery with microcredentials can be tied to financial rewards, leadership positions, and more. Last, when done well, creating microcredential tracks builds toward the future, as schools create in-house resources for professional development—through content and master educators—rather than relying on external resources.

Virginia Beach Public Schools, as an illustration, has developed a robust approach to microcredentialing. Teachers can embark on tracks such as

- Culturally responsive practices.
- Language literacy.
- Performance-based assessment.
- Personalized learning.
- Leading professional learning.
- Recognizing and understanding gifted learners.
- Leading teams.

Chelyse Miller, a professional learning specialist and former math teacher for Virginia Beach Schools, remarked that microcredentials "honored me as a professional and I learned through creating a product or portfolio. When I received notification that I earned the microcredential, I felt proud of myself and the work I put into it. It validated me."

Every educator has different needs for efficacy. One-size-fits-all PD is a misnomer; most programs are one-size-fits-a-few-and-constricts-the-rest. Letting teachers invest skill development in what matters to them, such as with microcredentialing, is a key way to increase autonomy *and* efficacy.

Strategy #5: Well-Trained Mentors

Last year, I was curious about how our mentor system worked in our district. Having been asked to be a mentor a couple times, to my knowledge the system basically went like this: A veteran teacher was asked to be a mentor. If the person agreed, then they become the mentor. End of process. But then I found out that we *did* have a mentor handbook (tsk, tsk, Chase, for not doing the homework). After a whole lot of searching, I finally found the handbook in a random digital file on Google Drive—a PDF of a hand-copied document—and realized this thing was *ancient*. Case in point, it had suggestions like "be sure to show your mentee where the designated smoking sections of school are." Our mentor program, like many schools, was more an idea than an up-to-date system of support.

Mentor teachers are often required by some schools. But how robust is your mentor program? Research by Smith and Ingersoll (2004) established that there are three main levels of mentor support:

- Level 1: An assigned mentor and supportive communication with administrators.
- Level 2: Level 1 plus seminar trainings for beginning teachers and collaboration with other teachers on instruction.
- Level 3: Level 2 plus participation in an external teacher network and logistical support like reduced number of preparations.

Their research found that 56 percent of new teachers receive Level 1 support, 29 percent receive Level 2, but less than 1 percent receive Level 3 support. The level of support predicted that the probability of turnover after the first year was 41 percent for teachers who had no induction or mentorship, 39 percent for teachers receiving Level 1 support, 27 percent for teachers with Level 2 support, and 18 percent for teachers with Level 3 support. The greater the support, the greater the efficacy and, thus, the greater the likelihood teachers stay.

Other questions to consider: How well-trained are your mentors (or are they trained at all)? How does your selection process work (e.g., good teachers don't always make good mentors)? One great place to start is training mentors on the four roots of efficacy. Not only can you train mentors on using Efficacy Ladders—you can use them to develop *mentor* efficacy. List out all the things a new hire should know and be able to do by the end of a designated year. Then work backward, breaking this knowledge and these skills into logical, sequenced checkpoints. Many effective mentor programs provide these monthly checklists that mentors must go through with mentees. In addition to these checklists, consider adding inter-coaching and intra-coaching reflection questions and the Efficacy Survey from Appendix C to assess needs (but maybe consider scrapping the "smoking section" advice).

Let's also remember that efficacy is context dependent. Just because a teacher has veteran experience doesn't mean they don't also need support. Consider giving all new staff a mentor for at least the first year even if they are a veteran—if nothing else, it gives them a designated person who can help them figure out logistical differences like the specific learning management systems, what district supports exist, and which of the *many* copy machines actually works.

Strategy #6: High Fives and Helping Hands

Finally, the low-budget, low-effort strategy to offer is to be proactive with *high fives and helpings hands*. Every educator needs more of two things: recognition for their hard work and a leader who helps them solve problems. Multiple studies have found that teacher efficacy rises when principals provide individualized support, listen, help solve problems, encourage innovation, and are perceived as helpful (Blase & Blase, 2000; Ross & Gray, 2006). We also know that efficacy rises when workers attend to positive emotions (Buonomo et al., 2019).

A key distinction is asking yourself, "Am I *reactive* or *proactive* with my recognition and support? Do I wait until someone seems frustrated or burned out before I offer them help or praise? Or do I have an active system of checking in with each staff member before they are stressed and struggling?"

I recommend building habits for affirmation and offering support. For example, in my previous school, administrators hosted monthly "climate meetings" where they would buy food and teachers could pop in on their lunch break. Teachers had open conversations about what is going well—sharing acknowledgments of colleagues and positive moments—as well as what wasn't—thus creating a window for administrators to learn how to better support.

Or simply set a weekly habit like "Gratituesday" and start every Tuesday writing a quick note of gratitude or affirmation for a staff member. How about "Fix It Friday," where you check in with a different staff member each Friday to offer problem-solving support? Shall I keep going with day-of-the-week wordplay? You get the idea: One small weekly habit is better than a large burst of motivation with no follow-through.

The Kids Need You

I'm not going to go as far as saying that your staff are your *children*—that would be unhealthy and weird. But there is something to thinking about your staff as kids who are learning to walk, each in their own way. They may *want* to take risks, but do the conditions of your culture allow it? Do they have clear structure and steps to take? Do they have agency to try it their own way? Do they have models and benchmarks of success—long-term and short-term? Most of all, do they see you, the leader, as a support who encourages their risks, celebrates their progress, gives feedback for growth, and cheers and dusts them off when they fall and fail?

Sure, they might stumble and figure it out on their own. But they'll figure it out faster (and stay longer) in a culture that encourages and supports efficacy growth with clear application of mastery experiences, social modeling, verbal persuasion, and positive emotions. Why let your staff stumble in isolation? Why stick to old comfort zones of staff development that don't stretch us for new growth? Why take baby steps when we can leap and launch to new heights?

Conclusion:
It Starts with One Spark

Beside me in my desk is a stack of letters. Notes—some pages long, some a few words, some handwritten in pricey cards, some scrawled on scraps of paper. Almost all of them are from former students describing how our time together changed their lives. Almost all of them are reflections from the most fulfilling experience of my life: creating and developing a positive psychology class for high school students.

For over a decade, I walked alongside teenagers as we explored the science of well-being—gratitude, purpose, mindfulness, engagement, optimism, and relatedness. I tinkered and tweaked lessons and experiences, vigilant about *living* the research and not just discussing them. But, among the many moments of joy and meaning, among the awards for the course and the reduced failure rates of the "at-risk" students who took part, one assignment, the final project, stands as the essence of everything this class—and this book—is about. One assignment that took one whole day and was just one sentence long: make strangers smile.

For a couple days leading up to the final project, students would break into groups and start brainstorming all the ways they could make complete strangers smile. Then, we would pile onto a bus one morning, drive to downtown Kalamazoo, Michigan, and I would release these teenagers into the wild.

I learned a lot on this trip. First, I learned that teenagers are super-creative. They came up with some wild ideas, and some of them were actually legal. They concocted ways to bring giant vats of hot chocolate on snowy days and hand them out on the frigid sidewalks. They convinced the local florist to donate flowers for them to hand out. They raised money to buy socks and toiletries to give to those less fortunate on the streets. But, among these many ideas, I learned that it was the simplest action that had the most profound effect: my students would change the world, over and over, simply by handing out positive notes to strangers. Index cards with affirmations—handwriting imperfect, grammar and spelling all janky. I have countless memories of watching these interactions, but one stands out the most.

We were in the downtown Kalamazoo library one day when a group of my students came sprinting up to me, sobbing. After my initial panic of "Stranger danger! What happened?!" they assured me everything was OK. Then they told me what happened.

They were on a mission to find the most miserable person they could. Seriously. Overachievers on the assignment, they were scanning the library for the least happy person. That guy? Nah, too smiley. Her? Nope. Seems OK. Then they spotted her: a lady who looked miserable. They found the perfect person. Now they needed the perfect note.

They flipped through all their notes and *boom* they found it. They awkwardly walked up to the lady, silently slid her the letter, scampered away, and then looked back. To their horror, they saw the lady start bawling in the library. They panicked, thinking they've offended her. They rushed up to apologize and, as they went to say sorry, she threw her arms out for a hug.

She cried into the shoulders of my students, these strangers.

Then she told them why.

She had suffered a miscarriage. One month prior to receiving this note, she lost her child. And every day for the last month she questioned her desire to live. Why should she keep going? Why would life punish her like this? What was the point?

But then she told my students that this note, to her, was a sign from God to not give up. The note said four words: It will get better.

Four words on an index card may have saved this human being's life. And it rippled out to my students. One of my students came back from the field trip and said, "Mr. Mielke, never in my life have I felt like I had purpose. Until today." And this story ignites a reminder to me, to shine to you and remind all of us of a critical idea:

We so often overcomplicate what it means to make a difference in our schools. We think it has to be the perfect, drama-free day. Enthusiastic embracing of massive reform. Skyrocketing test scores. But it's the simplest interactions that mean the most to the people around us—minor moments aggregating into profound influence. It's smiling at the colleague who hasn't seen a smile all day. Listening to someone who hasn't felt heard in months. Standing beside someone with support when they don't feel strong enough to stand on their own.

And, no matter what your role in education, no matter how much "power" you have in your job, you get to *choose* to create these moments—these sparks—every single day. This book has given you a lot of ideas for igniting change in your organization to help people be more effective and affective, but don't get overwhelmed by doing all the things all at once. Start with tomorrow. Set a Compass Mindset of how you want people to feel when they enter your school. Then, foster curiosity, compassion, and creativity whenever and however you can to help them feel that way—one smile, one listening ear, one offer of support, one spark at a time.

The work of education is hard, yet I'm convinced that no other profession changes lives the way it can. And I have the notes in my desk to prove it.

It will get better. Because we get to make it better. Every day.

It only takes one spark to ignite a flame—to illuminate a new path for education. That spark is you.

Appendix A:
Sample Burnout Inventory

Identify how you've felt with your work. Use the key below to help make your decisions. After each section, add up your totals for your score (the higher the number, the higher the burnout in that category).

1 = Rarely (few times a year); **2 = Occasionally** (monthly); **3 = Often** (weekly); **4 = Frequently** (every 2–3 days); **5 = Constantly** (daily)

Exhaustion

	1	2	3	4	5
I feel drained by my work.					
I feel I don't have enough time or energy to complete my tasks.					
I am frustrated at work.					

Exhaustion Score: _____

Cynicism

	1	2	3	4	5
I feel easily irritated by others at work (colleagues, supervisors, students, parents).					
I've become more cynical or callous toward others or toward my organization.					
I don't have the energy or desire to handle interpersonal conflicts.					

Cynicism Score: _____

Inefficacy

	1	2	3	4	5
I am failing at accomplishing my goals as an educator.					
I don't feel like the work I do matters.					
The skills I have aren't enough to tackle all the challenges I face.					

Inefficacy Score: _____

Optional Questions:

What is one thing that, if it were taken off your workload, would instantly allow you to do your job better?

How do you predict your burnout levels might change over the next six months?

Appendix B:
The Whats

To draw insights or meaning out of an experience, work through these phases of discussion:

What?

State *facts* of the situation.

- What did you see?
- What did you hear?
- What do you do?
- What is the data?

So What?

Reflect on the *meaning* from the facts you just noted.

- What do you think ____ means?
- What do you think caused _____? What was the effect?
- What does ____ suggest about an individual's experience? Or a group's experience?
- How does this relate to life/teaching/another context?

Now What?

Decide on specific action steps to turn this learning into action.

- Based on _____ , what is one specific action we can take to apply this insight?
- What is your next immediate move—what will you do in the next day/week as a result?
- What goal do you now have after _____?
- What support will you need to achieve this goal?
- How will you measure your progress/growth of this goal?

Appendix C: Efficacy Survey

For each of the following, mark if you Strongly Disagree (SD), Disagree (D), Agree (A), or Strongly Agree (SA).

Classroom Management

	SD	D	A	SA
I am able to handle classroom disruptions quickly and efficiently.				
If a student becomes disruptive to the learning of others, I am confident in handling it.				
I have clear routines and procedures that maximize learning in my classroom.				
My transitions between learning experiences are quick and effective.				
When I redirect students or request a change in their behavior, they follow my request.				
I am able to prevent misbehaviors or distractions from disrupting the learning of others.				
When my initial efforts to curb misbehaviors fail, I have a variety of other skills to try.				
I can get through to even the most challenging students.				

Engagement

	SD	D	A	SA
Students are engaged in the learning experiences throughout my lessons.				
I have a variety of strategies to help students focus on their learning.				
I am able to keep my students attentive and curious during direct instruction.				
I pace my lessons well to keep students from losing focus.				
I help students think and learn independently.				
I help students think and learn collaboratively.				

Instruction

	SD	D	A	SA
My lessons are rigorous and stretch students to grow.				
I have a variety of strategies for appropriately differentiating learning to reach all my students.				
I ask good questions that encourage critical thinking.				
If students are struggling to understand, I can pivot my teaching to help them get back on track.				
When students succeed in my class, it's because I have worked hard to design and deliver effective teaching.				
I am competent and skillful in responding to difficult questions.				

Assessment

	SD	D	A	SA
I ask questions that help me understand clearly if students are learning what I want them to learn.				
If students do not perform as expected on an assessment, I know how to adjust my teaching to help them succeed.				
If students don't perform as expected on an assessment, I can easily diagnose whether the learning experience was at an appropriate level for them.				
I have a variety of strategies to make student learning visible.				
I know how to differentiate my assessment for diverse types of learners and student abilities.				

Culture and Community

	SD	D	A	SA
My students feel safe and respected in my class because I work hard to create this culture.				
I can help students believe they are capable of learning hard things.				
Students enjoy my classroom because I have strategies for making it joyful and meaningful.				
I am effective in helping parents support their child's learning at home.				
I know how to help my students find motivation and value learning.				
My classroom atmosphere is well organized, focused, and productive.				
My work and efforts improve the culture of our school.				

Source: Mielke, C. (2021). The critical element of self-efficacy. *Educational Leadership, 79*(3), 14–19.

Appendix D:
The D-Stress Strategies

Stress is a part of life. If we can't be stress *resistant*, we should develop skills to be stress *resilient*. Almost every stress management strategy falls under what I call the "5 D-Stressors." Learn them all (or teach them), then practice applying the right strategy to the right situation.

Distract

Create physical, cognitive, and/or emotional distance from a stressor.

Why it works: Due to homeostasis, our body naturally wants to return to a state of balance when our stress levels rise. If we can create time and space away from a stressor, we let time function as a regulator.

Key ideas:

1. Distraction is best when (a) the stressor isn't likely to return (someone cuts us off in traffic) or (b) emotional hijacking is high (we are heated in an argument).
2. Distraction doesn't address the stressor, so it is often over-used and can turn into a habit (e.g., procrastination). We can't, for example, distract away from things like deadlines or financial debt.

3. If we tend to ruminate—or we experience a lot of chronic stress—distraction isn't always as effective. It's not always easy to "stop worrying about it."

4. Not all distraction methods are equally effective. For example, scrolling social media as a distraction can sometimes *increase* stress (e.g., doomscrolling). Conversely, a distraction like exercise is physically stressful, but because it is acute and controlled, it trains our body to handle stress better in the future.

Examples:

There are three main routes of distraction:

- Thought redirect
  - Participating in a hobby
  - Reading a book
- Emotion redirect
  - Watching a funny movie
  - Taking a relaxing bath
- Physical redirect
  - Exercising
  - Going for a walk

Deal with the Stressor

Use problem-solving strategies to reduce the stressor.

Why it works: When we work to solve a problem, not only does our positive action increase our resilience, but we also learn new coping strategies for similar situations. And, of course, if we address the stressor, we have less stress.

Key ideas:

1. If our attempt to deal with the stressor fails, we can sometimes get more frustrated. So, this strategy works best when we pair it with other methods (e.g., disputing negative thoughts, developing mindfulncss).

2. Consider dealing with the stressor as a process—it might take a few rounds of trying new things, learning from the mistake, and tweaking strategies.
3. Not all stressors can be "fixed," but we can still apply problem-solving strategies to come up with new coping approaches.

Typical steps:

You'll notice these steps mirror the Creativity Mindset steps. These steps can be even more effective when we research or invite others in, especially those who have success with similar problems.

1. Identify the real problem.
2. Brainstorm solutions.
3. Analyze best methods to try.
4. Identify potential obstacles and how you will overcome them.
5. Take action steps (what, when, where, how).
6. Re-evaluate to see if new strategies are needed.

Discuss

Process the stressor to reduce rumination and move forward.

Why it works: Putting our stressors and emotions into words activates the prefrontal cortex, which can reduce activity in the amygdala. It can also provide us insights for reframing the stressor or taking new action.

Key ideas:

1. Discussing works well when our rumination is high and/or other methods aren't helping.
2. Too much processing can sometimes have an opposite effect, increasing our stress as we "sit in the mud." So, aim for a high progress-to-process ratio. *Process* means talking through or venting about the problem. *Progress* means identifying what you will do or think differently to move forward from the stressor. For example, if talking about a frustration with a colleague, limit your venting (process) to 30 percent of your time. Spend the rest of the time talking about actions steps for moving forward (progress).

3. Choose the right people to discuss your stressors. Some people may attempt to fix our problems and give unsolicited advice rather than listening fully. Others might "stress steal" and make our stressor about themselves.

Examples:

- Writing or journaling
- Talking with a mentor, friend, or partner
- Prayer or spiritual practice

Dispute Negative Thoughts

Use mental reframes to reduce rumination and resentment.

Why it works: Our thoughts can increase or intensify our stress levels. *Disputation* is when we recognize an unhealthy thought pattern and combat it with a reframe. This mental reframe helps us see our circumstances more logically and increase our optimism that we can handle stress in the future.

Key ideas:

We all have a metacognitive style for thinking about stressors that we have developed for decades. Disputation is one of the most common strategies used in cognitive behavioral therapy, which means it is effective, but it takes a lot of work to change.

Examples:

Thought Pattern	Example	Disputation
Black/white thinking (believing something is all one way or another)	"That lesson was a disaster."	**Finding the middle** "Although there were parts of that lesson that were rough, students really understood the main idea of the story."

(*continued on next page*)

Thought Pattern	Example	Disputation
Personalizing (putting on the blame on oneself)	"It's all my fault our fundraiser fell short."	**Contextualizing** "I could have tried some different ideas, but this is my first time leading this committee. I'm still learning, so I need to be kind to myself."
Catastrophizing (taking one stressor and blowing it up to a wider category)	"Teaching is terrible."	**Specify the stressor** "I'm overwhelmed by the meetings and mandates lately, but I still love the work I do with my kids."
Making it permanent (assuming a stressor will always be there)	"These kids are never going to get this."	**Attach the temporary** "Some of these kids are struggling *right now*, but I will try a new strategy tomorrow."

Develop Mindfulness

Use focused, nonjudgmental attention practices to increase equanimity.

Why it works: There are many reasons why mindfulness helps us become more stress resilient:

- Practicing nonjudgmental thinking can detach our emotional response to an event.
- Deep breathing activates the parasympathetic nervous system, reducing our fight/flight/freeze response and our stress levels.
- Focused attention helps us shift thoughts from rumination.
- Thought-noting engages the prefrontal cortex, reducing activity in the amygdala (which triggers our fight/flight/freeze response).

Key Ideas:

1. Mindfulness is like exercise; there are countless variations, each serving a different purpose. Just as one workout doesn't change physical health, one meditation isn't enough. But, also like exercise, even a little bit of practice each day can improve our health.

2. You don't have to meditate. Educators don't always have time for full meditation, but it can be helpful to find "mindful moments" throughout our days. Check out mindfulness guru Thich Nhat Hanh's (1992) book *Peace Is Every Step* for great examples of mindfulness practices that don't require lengthy meditation.

Examples:

- Yoga
- Meditation
- Mindfulness-based stress reduction
- Deep breathing exercises

Resources:

- **Guided Meditation**
  — Mindful.org (https://www.mindful.org)
  — Meditation Oasis (https://www.meditationoasis.com/podcast)
  — Palouse Mindfulness (https://palousemindfulness.com)
- **Apps**
  — Simple Habit
  — Aura Headspace Calm
- **Yoga**
  — Funky Buddha Yoga (https://yogahothouse.com/yoga-videos/)
  — Do Yoga with Me (www.doyogawithme.com)

References

American Tarantula & Animals. (2022, October 8). 8 main reasons why snakes eat themselves. Author. https://www.atshq.org/do-snakes-eat-themselves/

Arens, A. K., &, Morin, A. J. S. (2016). Relations between teachers' emotional exhaustion and students' educational outcomes. *Journal of Educational Psychology, 108*, 800–813.

Asensio-Martínez, N., Leiter, M. P., Gascón, S., Gumuchian, S., Masluk, B., Herrera-Mercadal, P., Albesa, A., & García-Campayo, J. (2017, September 7). Value congruence, control, sense of community and demands as determinants of burnout syndrome among hospitality workers. *International Journal of Occupational Safety and Ergonomics, 25*(2), 287–295. https://doi.org/10.1080/10803548.2017.1367558

Atalay, M. O., Aydemir, P., & Acuner, T. (2022). The influence of emotional exhaustion on organizational cynicism: The sequential mediating effect of organizational identification and trust in organization. SAGE Open. https://doi.org/10.1177/21582440221093343

Bakker, A. B., & van Wingerden, J. (2020). Do personal resources and strengths use increase work engagement? The effects of a training intervention. *Journal of Occupational Health Psychology*. http://doi.org/10.1037/ocp0000266

Bartlett, L. (2021, August 26). Will the pandemic drive teachers out of the profession? What one study says. *Education Week*. https://www.edweek.org/teaching-learning/opinion-will-the-pandemic-drive-teachers-out-of-the-profession-what-one-study-says/2021/08

Beaudan, E. (2006). Making change last: How to get beyond change fatigue. *Ivey Business Journal*. https://web.archive.org/web/20060329010354id_/http://www.iveybusinessjournal.com/view_article.asp?intArticle_ID=608

Beausaert, S., Froehlich, D. E., Devos, C., & Riley, P. (2016). Effects of support on stress and burnout in school principals. *Educational Research, 58*(4), 347–365. doi: 10.1080/00131881.2016.1220810

Bedeian, A. G. (2007). Even if the tower is "ivory," it isn't "white:" Understanding the consequences of faculty cynicism. *Academy of Management Learning & Education, 6*(1), 9–32.

Bellis, R. (2015, September 25). Why it's so hard to pay attention, explained by science. *Fast Company*. https://www.fastcompany.com/3051417/why-its-so-hard-to-pay-attention-explained-by-science

Beltman, S., Mansfield, C., & Price, A. (2011). Thriving not just surviving: A review of research on teacher resilience. *Educational Research Review*. 10.1016/j.edurev.2011.09.001.

Bill and Melinda Gates Foundation. (2012). *Primary sources 2012: America's teachers on the teaching profession*. Scholastic.

Blanchet, M. (2022). What does trust look like in schools? *Edutopia*. https://www.edutopia.org/article/what-does-trust-look-school

Blase, J., & Blase, R. R. (2000, August 30). *Empowering teachers: What successful principals do* (2nd ed.). Corwin.

Buonomo, I., Fiorilli, C., & Benevene, P. (2019). The impact of emotions and hedonic balance on teachers' self-efficacy: Testing the bouncing back effect of positive emotions. *Frontiers in Psychology, 10*, Article 1670. https://doi.org/10.3389/fpsyg.2019.01670

Caposey, P. J. (2022, March 15). Real actions school leaders can take to support teachers. *Edutopia*. https://www.edutopia.org/article/real-actions-school-leaders-can-take-support-teachers

Carbaugh, E. M., McCullough, L., Raftery, M., & Linaburg, E. (2022). *Building educator capacity through microcredentials*. ASCD.

Carr, S. (2022, January 5). Public schools are struggling to retain black teachers. These ex-teachers explain why. *TIME*. https://time.com/6130991/black-teachers-resigning/

CDC. (2016, January 1). 1 in 3 adults don't get enough sleep. Author. https://www.cdc.gov/media/releases/2016/p0215-enough-sleep.html

CDC. (n.d.). School connectedness. https://www.cdc.gov/healthyyouth/protective/school_connectedness.htm

Christakis, N. A., & Fowler, J. H. (2009). *Connected: The amazing power of social networks and how they shape our lives*. HarperCollins.

Churches, R. (2020). *Supporting teachers through the school workload reduction toolkit*. Education Development Trust. https://assets.publishing.service.gov.uk/

Clear, J. (2018). *Atomic habits: An easy and proven way to build good habits and break bad ones*. National Geographic Books.

Collins, S. K., & Collins, K. S. (2002). Micromanagement—A costly management style. *Radiology management, 24*(6), 32–35.

Deci, E. L., & Flaste, R. (1996, August 1). *Why we do what we do: Understanding self-motivation*. Penguin.

Deloitte Insights. (2020). *The social enterprise at work: Paradox as a path forward*. 2020 Deloitte Global Human Capital Trends. Deloitte.

Dicke, T., Parker, P. D., Marsh, H. W., Kunter, M., Schmech, A., & Leutner, D. (2014). Self-efficacy in classroom management, classroom disturbances, and emotional exhaustion: A moderated mediation analysis of teacher candidates. *Journal of Educational Psychology 106*(2), 569–583. doi: 10.1037/a0035504

Digestive Health Team. (2021, December 27). Is being 'hangry' really a thing—or just an excuse? *Cleveland Clinic*. https://health.clevelandclinic.org/is-being-hangry-really-a-thing-or-just-an-excuse/

Dileberti, M. K., & Schwartz, H. L. (2021). Stress was leading reason teachers quit before pandemic, and COVID-19 has made matters worse. RAND Education and Labor. https://www.rand.org/news/press/2021/02/22.html

Dixon, R. D., Griffin, A. R., & Teoh, M. B. (2019). *If you listen, we will stay: Why teachers of color leave and how to disrupt teacher turnover.* Education Trust & Teach Plus.

Donaldson, S. I., Lee, J. Y., & Donaldson, S. I. (2019). Evaluating positive psychology interventions at work: A systematic review and meta-analysis. *International Journal of Applied Positive Psychology, 4*(3), 113–134. https://doi.org/10.1007/s41042-019-00021-8

DuFour, R., DuFour, R., Eaker, R., Many, T. W., & Mattos, M. (2016, May 18). *Learning by doing: A handbook for professional learning communities at work (An actionable guide to implementing the PLC process and effective teaching methods)* (3rd ed.). Solution Tree.

Eddy, C. L., Huang, F. L., Cohen, D. R., Baker, K. M., Edwards, K. C., Herman, K. C., & Reinke, W. L. (2020). Does teacher emotional exhaustion and efficacy predict student discipline sanctions? *School Psychology Review, 49*(3), 239–255.

Education Week. (2022). *1st annual Merrimack College teacher survey: 2022 results.* EdWeek Research Center.

EL Education. (2015). *Relational trust in schools.* Author. https://eleducation.org/resources/relational-trust-in-schools

Elliot, A. J., & Sheldon, K. M. (1998). Avoidance personal goals and the personality illness relationship. *Journal of Personality and Social Psychology, 75,* 1282–1299.

Emmons, R. A. (1999). *The psychology of ultimate concerns: Motivation and spirituality in personality.* Guilford.

Epstein, R. (1999). *Encyclopedia of Creativity, 1*(1) 759–756.

Epstein, R. (2011). *Encyclopedia of Creativity, 2*(1) 480–487.

Farris-Berg, K., & Dirkswager, E. J. (2012, October 10). *Trusting teachers with school success: What happens when teachers call the shots.* R&L Education.

Flink, C., Boggiano, A. K., & Barrett, M. (1990). Controlling teaching strategies: Undermining children's self-determination and performance. *Journal of Personality and Social Psychology, 59*(5), 916–924. https://doi.org/10.1037/0022-3514.59.5.916

Gallup. (2020). *Gallup's perspective on employee burnout: Causes and cures.* Author. https://www.gallup.com/workplace/282659/employee-burnout-perspective-paper.aspx

Garcia, E., & Weiss, E. (2019, March 26). *The teacher shortage is real, large and growing, and worse than we thought.* The Perfect Storm in the Teacher Labor Market series. Economic Policy Institute. https://www.epi.org/publication/the-teacher-shortage-is-real-large-and-growing-and-worse-than-we-thought-the-first-report-in-the-perfect-storm-in-the-teacher-labor-market-series/

Garland, E. L., Fredrickson, B., Kring, A. M., Johnson, D. P., Meyer, P. S., & Penn, D. L. (2010). Upward spirals of positive emotions counter downward spirals of negativity: Insights from the broaden-and-build theory and affective neuroscience on the treatment of emotion dysfunctions and deficits in psychopathology. *Clinical Psychology Review, 30*(7), 849–864. https://doi.org/10.1016/j.cpr.2010.03.002

Geller, A. (2022, January 31). Should you cancel teacher data team meetings? You might be surprised. *SmartBrief.* https://corp.smartbrief.com/original/2021/09/should-you-cancel-teacher-data-team-meetings-you-might-be-surprised

Goleman, D. (2006). *Emotional intelligence: Why it can matter more than IQ* (10th ed.). Bantam Books.

Greenberg, M. T., Brown J. L., & Abenavoli, R. M. (2016). *Teacher stress and health effects on teachers, students, and schools.* Edna Bennett Pierce Prevention Research Center, Pennsylvania State University.

Gundlach, H. (2022, February 28). Higher salaries might attract teachers but pay isn't one of the top 10 reasons for leaving. https://phys.org/news/2022-02-higher-salaries-teachers-isnt.html

Hanh, T. M. (1992). *Peace is every step: The path of mindfulness in everyday life.* Random House.

Hargreaves, A. (2003). *Teaching in the knowledge society: Education in the age of insecurity.* Teachers College Press.

Hattie, J. (2008). *Visible learning* (1st ed.). Routledge.

Herzberg, F. (1964). The motivation-hygiene concept and problems of manpower. *Personnel Administration* (27), 3–7.

Hodges, B. T. (2022, April 6). Why appreciating teachers is more important than you think. Gallup.com. https://news.gallup.com/opinion/gallup/210041/why-appreciating-teachers-important-think.aspx

Holzberger, D., Philipp, A., & Kunter, M. (2013). How teachers' self-efficacy is related to instructional quality: A longitudinal analysis. *Journal of Educational Psychology 105*(3), 774–786. doi: 10.1037/a0032191

Jerabek, I. (2018, November 24). *From neglect to burnout: New study emphasizes importance of employee appreciation.* PsychTests. https://www.prweb.com/releases/from_neglect_to_burnout_new_study_emphasizes_importance_of_employee_appreciation/prweb15918967.htm

Judge, T. A., & Bono, J. E. (2001). Relationship of core self-evaluations traits—self-esteem, generalized self-efficacy, locus of control, and emotional stability—with job satisfaction and job performance: A meta-analysis. *Journal of Applied Psychology, 86*(1), 80–92.

Karadağ, E., Kiliçoğu, G., & Yilmaz, D. (2014, March 6). Organizational cynicism, school culture, and academic achievement: The study of structural equation modeling. *Educational Sciences: Theory & Practice.* https://doi.org/10.12738/estp.2014.1.1640

Kasser, T., & Ryan, R. M. (1996). Further examining the American dream: Differential correlates of intrinsic and extrinsic goals. *Personality and Social Psychology Bulletin, 22,* 280–287.

Katz, V. (2018). Teacher retention: Evidence to inform policy [Press release]. https://education.virginia.edu/policy-virginia

Kieschnick, W., & Kieschnick, M. (2020). *Breaking bold: Dare to defy the tyranny of trends and live the relationship habits of a master educator.* International Center for Leadership in Education.

King, L. A., & Emmons, R. A. (1991). Psychological, physical, and interpersonal correlates of emotional expressiveness, conflict, and control. *European Journal of Personality, 5,* 131–150.

Klug, H. J., & Maier, G. W. (2014). Linking goal progress and subjective well-being: A meta-analysis. *Journal of Happiness Studies, 16*(1), 37–65. doi:10.1007/s10902-013-9493-0

Klusmann, U., Richter, D., & Lüdtke, O. (2016). Teachers' emotional exhaustion is negatively related to students' achievement: Evidence from a large-scale assessment study. *Journal of Educational Psychology, 108*(8), 1193–1203.

Knight, J. (2017). *The impact cycle: What instructional coaches should do to foster powerful improvements in teaching.* Corwin.

Kurtz, H. (2022, June 9). *A profession in crisis: Findings from a national teacher survey.* EdWeek Research Center. https://www.edweek.org/research-center /reports/teaching-profession-in-crisis-national-teacher-survey

Leithwood, K. A. (2006). *Teacher working conditions that matter: Evidence for change.* Elementary Teachers' Federation of Ontario.

Leroy, N., Bressoux, P., Sarrazin, P., & Trouilloud, D. (2007). Impact of teachers' implicit theories and perceived pressures on the establishment of an autonomy supportive climate. *European Journal of Psychology of Education, 22*, 529–545.

Li, S., & Chen, Y. (2018, July 27). The relationship between psychological contract breach and employees' counterproductive work behaviors: The mediating effect of organizational cynicism and work alienation. *Frontiers in Psychology, 9.* https://doi.org/10.3389/fpsyg.2018.01273

Li, X., Meng, X., Li, H., Yang, J., & Yuan, J. (2017). The impact of mood on empathy for pain: Evidence from an EEG study. *Psychophysiology, 54*(9), 1311–1322. doi:10.1111/psyp.12882

Linden, D. J. (2012, April 24). *The compass of pleasure: How our brains make fatty foods, orgasm, exercise, marijuana, generosity, vodka, learning, and gambling feel so good* (illustrated ed.). Penguin Books.

Manne, K. (2012, December 12). Leadership can reduce employee cynicism, increase engagement. University at Buffalo. https://www.buffalo.edu/news/releases/2012 /12/13855.html

Martin, A. J., & Collie, R. J. (2018). Teacher–student relationships and students' engagement in high school: Does the number of negative and positive relationships with teachers matter? *Journal of Educational Psychology.* DOI: 10.1037 /edu0000317

Maslach, C., & Leiter, M. P. (2000, January 21). *The truth about burnout: How organizations cause personal stress and what to do about it* (1st ed.). Jossey-Bass.

McGonigal, K. (2016, May 10). *The upside of stress: Why stress is good for you, and how to get good at it.* Avery.

McKee, A. (2016). If you can't empathize with your employees, you'd better learn to. *Harvard Business Review.* https://hbr.org/2016/11/if-you-cant-empathize-with -your-employees-youd-better-learn-to

Mcmahon, S. D., Martinez, A., Espelage, D., Rose, C., Reddy, L. A., Lane, K., Anderman, E. M., Reynolds, C. R., Jones, A., & Brown, V. (2014, June 29). Violence directed against teachers: Results from a national survey. *Psychology in the Schools, 51*(7), 753–766. https://doi.org/10.1002/pits.21777

Meredith, C., Schaufeli, W., Struyve, C., Vandecandelaere, M., Gielen, S., & Kyndt, E. (2019, October 13). 'Burnout contagion' among teachers: A social network approach. *Journal of Occupational and Organizational Psychology, 93*(2), 328–352. https://doi.org/10.1111/joop.12296

Mielke, C. (2019). *The burnout cure: Learning to love teaching again.* ASCD.

Miller, C. C. (n.d.). How to be more empathetic. *New York Times.* https://www .nytimes.com/guides/year-of-living-better/how-to-be-more-empathetic

Miller, S. (2008). Criminal defense counsel ponders "hungry for meatballs" defense. Skala Miller Law. https://www.skalamillerlaw.com/blog/2018/03/criminal -defense-counsel-ponders-hungry-for-meatballs-defense/

Moss, J. (2021, September 28). The burnout epidemic: The rise of chronic stress and how we can fix it. *Harvard Business Review.*

National Center for Education Statistics. (2003). *Schools and staffing survey.* U.S. Department of Education.

Nguyen, T. D., Lam, C. B., & Bruno, P. (2022). Is there a national teacher shortage? A systematic examination of reports of teacher shortages in the United States. *EdWorkingPaper, 22*(631).

Novotney, A. (2022). The science of creativity: Use these empirically backed tips to capture your next big idea. American Psychological Association. https://www .apa.org/gradpsych/2009/01/creativity

O'Brennan, L., Pas, E., & Bradshaw, C. (2017, June 1). Multilevel examination of burnout among high school staff: Importance of staff and school factors. *School Psychology Review, 46*(2), 165–176. https://doi.org/10.17105/spr-2015-0019.v46-2

Ozdemir, Y. (2007). The role of classroom management efficacy in predicting teacher burnout. *World Academy of Science, Engineering and Technology International Journal of Educational and Pedagogical Sciences, 1*(11).

Pelletier, L. G., & Sharp, E. C. (2009, June 25). Administrative pressures and teachers' interpersonal behaviour in the classroom. *Theory and Research in Education, 7*(2), 174–183. https://doi.org/10.1177/1477878509104322

Pfitzner-Eden, F. (2016, October 19). Why do I feel more confident? Bandura's sources predict preservice teachers' latent changes in teacher self-efficacy. *Frontiers in Psychology, 7.* https://doi.org/10.3389/fpsyg.2016.01486

Pfrombeck, J., Doden, W., Grote, G., & Felerabend, A. (2020). A study of organizational cynicism and how it is affected by social exchange relationships at work. *Journal of Occupational and Organizational Psychology, 93*(3). https://doi.org/10.1111 /joop.12306

Pietarinen, J., Pyhältö, K., Haverinen, K., Leskinen, E., & Soini, T. (2021, July 2). Is individual- and school-level teacher burnout reduced by proactive strategies? *International Journal of School & Educational Psychology, 9*(4), 340–355. https:// doi.org/10.1080/21683603.2021.1942344

Power, R. A., & Pluess, M. (2015). Heritability estimates of the Big Five personality traits based on common genetic variants. *Translational Psychiatry, 5*(7). https:// doi.org/10.1038/tp.2015.96

Răducu, C. M., & Stănculescu, E. (2022, April 25). Teachers' burnout risk during the COVID-19 pandemic: Relationships with socio-contextual stress—A latent profile analysis. *Frontiers in Psychiatry, 13.* https://doi.org/10.3389/fpsyt.2022.870098

Reeves, D. B. (2011). *Finding your leadership focus: What matters most for student results.* Amsterdam University Press.

Rogers, M., Doan, L., & Dovigo, F. (2021). *Bound for burnout: Early childhood educators are swimming against a gendered, micromanaged tide.* University of New England. https://rune.une.edu.au/web/bitstream/1959.11/31757/1 /openpublished/BurnoutRogers2021JournalArticle.pdf

Ross, J. A., & Gray, P. (2006). Transformational leadership and teacher commitment to organizational values. The mediating effects of collective teacher efficacy. *School Effectiveness and School Improvement, 17*(2), 179–199.

Ross, J. A., Hogaboam-Gray, A., & Hannay, L. (2001, November). Effects of teacher efficacy on computer skills and computer cognitions of Canadian students in grades K–3. *Elementary School Journal, 102*(2), 141–156. https://doi.org /10.1086/499697

Roth, G., Assor, A., Kanat-Maymon, Y., & Kaplan, H. (2007). Autonomous motivation for teaching: How self-determined teaching may lead to self-determined learning. *Journal of Educational Psychology, 99*(4), 761–774. https://doi.org/10.1037/0022 -0663.99.4.761

Santoro, D. A. (2018, June 1). Is it burnout or demoralization? *Educational Leadership, 75*(9). https://www.ascd.org/el/articles/is-it-burnout-or-demoralization

Saphier, J. (2018). Let's get specific about how leaders can build trust. Learning Forward. https://learningforward.org/journal/december-2018-volume-39-no-6/lets-get-specific-about-how-leaders-can-build-trust/

Schmoker, M. (2016). *Leading with focus: Elevating the essentials for school and district improvement*. ASCD.

Schwab, R. L., & Iwanicki, E. F. (1982, February). Perceived role conflict, role ambiguity, and teacher burnout. *Educational Administration Quarterly, 18*(1), 60–74. https://doi.org/10.1177/0013161x82018001005

Seligman, M. E. P. (2004, January 5). *Authentic happiness: Using the new positive psychology to realize your potential for lasting fulfillment*. Atria Books.

Seppala, E., & King, M. (2021, August 27). Burnout at work isn't just about exhaustion. It's also about loneliness. *Harvard Business Review*. https://hbr.org/2017/06/burnout-at-work-isnt-just-about-exhaustion-its-also-about-loneliness

Sguera, F., Patient, D., Diehl, M., & Bobocel, R. (2021, September 24). Thank you for the bad news: Reducing cynicism in highly identified employees during adverse organizational change. *Journal of Occupational and Organizational Psychology, 95*(1), 90–130. https://doi.org/10.1111/joop.12369

Sheldon, K. M., & Elliot, A. J. (1999). Goal striving, need satisfaction, and longitudinal well-being: The self-concordance model. *Journal of Personality and Social Psychology, 76*(3), 482–497. doi:10.1037//0022-3514.76.3.482

Silani, G., Lamm, C., Ruff, C. C., & Singer, T. (2013). Right supramarginal gyrus is crucial to overcome emotional egocentricity bias in social judgments. *Journal of Neuroscience, 33*(39), 15466–15476.

Skaalvik, E., & Skaalvik, S. (2007). Dimensions of teacher self-efficacy and relations with strain factors, perceived collective teacher efficacy, and teacher burnout. *Journal of Educational Psychology, 99*(3), 611–625. https://doi.org/10.1037/0022-0663.99.3.611

Skaalvik, E., & Skaalvik, S. (2014, February). Teacher self-efficacy and perceived autonomy: Relations with teacher engagement, job satisfaction, and emotional exhaustion. *Psychological Reports, 114*(1), 68–77. https://doi.org/10.2466/14.02.pr0.114k14w0

Skaalvik, E., & Skaalvik, S. (2016). Teacher stress and teacher self-efficacy as predictors of engagement, emotional exhaustion, and motivation to leave the teaching profession. *Creative Education, 7*, 1785–1799.

Smith, T. M., & Ingersoll, R. M. (2004). What are the effects of induction and mentoring on beginning teacher turnover? *American Educational Research Journal, 41*(2).

Southwick, S. M., & Southwick, F. S. (2020, May 1). The loss of social connectedness as a major contributor to physician burnout. *JAMA Psychiatry, 77*(5), 449. https://doi.org/10.1001/jamapsychiatry.2019.4800

Sutcher, L., Darling-Hammond, L., & Carver-Thomas, D. (2016). *A coming crisis in teaching? Teacher supply, demand, and shortages in the U.S.* Learning Policy Institute.

Suttie, J. (2017, December 4). How a bad mood affects empathy in your brain. *Greater Good Magazine*. https://greatergood.berkeley.edu/article/item/how_a_bad_mood_affects_empathy_in_yoUr_brain

Syed, M., & Syed, A. (2013, July). Conscientiousness, neuroticism and burnout among healthcare employees. *International Journal of Academic Research in Business and Social Sciences, 3*(9), 467–477.

Szabo, E., & Jagodics, B. (2019, December). Teacher burnout in the light of workplace, organizational, and social factors. *Hungarian Educational Research Journal, 9*(3), 539–559. https://doi.org/10.1556/063.9.2019.3.44

Taxer, J. L., Becker-Kurz, B., & Frenzel, A. C. (2019). Do quality teacher–student relationships protect teachers from emotional exhaustion? The mediating role of enjoyment and anger. *Social Psychology of Education, 22*, 209–226.

Terhart, E. (2011). *Hattie, John. Visible learning. A synthesis of over 800 meta-analyses relating to achievement.* Routledge. Beltz.

Tschannen-Moran, M., & Hoy, A. W. (2007, August). The differential antecedents of self-efficacy beliefs of novice and experienced teachers. *Teaching and Teacher Education, 23*(6), 944–956. https://doi.org/10.1016/j.tate.2006.05.003

Tugade, M. M., Fredrickson, B. L., & Barrett, L. F. (2004). Psychological resilience and positive emotional granularity: Examining the benefits of positive emotions on coping and health. *Journal of Personality, 72*(6), 1161–1190. https://doi.org/10.1111/j.1467-6494.2004.00294.x

Venables, D. R. (2017). *Facilitating teacher teams and authentic PLCs: The human side of leading people, protocols, and practices.* ASCD.

Venkatesh, V., Ganster, D. C., Schuetz, S. W., & Sykes, T. A. (2021). Risks and rewards of conscientiousness during the COVID-19 pandemic. *Journal of Applied Psychology, 106*(5), 643–656.

Worth, J., & Van den Brande, J. (2020). *Teacher autonomy: How does it relate to job satisfaction and retention?* National Foundation for Educational Research.

Index

The letter *f* following a page locator denotes a figure.

About the Author

Chase Mielke is a veteran teacher and instructional coach, a nationally recognized speaker, and the author of ASCD's *The Burnout Cure: Learning to Love Teaching Again* and *Overcoming Educator Burnout (Quick Reference Guide)*.

A Michigan Teacher of the Year nominee and expert on teacher well-being, Chase delivers highly engaging, research-based, and practical keynotes and professional development workshops to schools and organizations across the world.

His work has been featured on CNN, *Greater Good Magazine*, and *Edutopia*. He hosts the *Educator Happy Hour* podcast and writes the Burnout Rx column for *EL Magazine*.

He resides with his family in Kalamazoo, Michigan, where he daydreams about fresh Expo markers and tries to keep his wild toddler from eating dog food and rocks.

Related ASCD Resources

At the time of publication, the following resources were available (ASCD stock numbers in parentheses).

The Burnout Cure: Learning to Love Teaching Again by Chase Mielke (#119004)

Compassionate Coaching: How to Help Educators Navigate Barriers to Professional Growth by Kathy Perret and Kenny McKee (#121017)

CRAFT Conversations for Teacher Growth: How to Build Bridges and Cultivate Expertise by Sally J. Zepeda, Lakesha Robinson Goff, and Stefanie W. Steele (#120001)

Educator Bandwidth: How to Reclaim Your Energy, Passion, and Time by Jane A. G. Kise and Ann C. Holm (#122019)

Forces of Influence: How Educators Can Leverage Relationships to Improve Practice by Fred Ende and Meghan Everette (#120009)

Overcoming Educator Burnout (Quick Reference Guide) by Chase Mielke (#QRG123016)

The Principal as Chief Empathy Officer: Creating a Culture Where Everyone Grows by Thomas R. Hoerr (#122030)

The Teacher's Principal: How School Leaders Can Support and Motivate Their Teachers by Jen Schwanke (#122035)

Trauma-Sensitive School Leadership: Building a Learning Environment to Support Healing and Success by Bill Ziegler, Dave Ramage, Andrea Parson, and Justin Foster (#122013)

For up-to-date information about ASCD resources, go to www.ascd .org. You can search the complete archives of *Educational Leadership* at www.ascd.org/el. To contact us, send an email to member@ascd.org or call 1-800-933-2723 or 703-578-9600.